A Golfer's Guide to Christianity

Walking the Fairways of Life by Faith

A Golfer's Guide to Christianity

ISBN-13: 978-1533347169

ISBN-10: 1533347166

A Golfer's Guide to Christianity

Walking the Fairways of Life by Faith

Michael Duncan

Other books by Michael Duncan

Starting Out: A Study Guide for New Believers

The Discipling Church: Encouraging, Equipping and Empowering the Body of Christ (With Tony Marino, Dr. Jeff Klick and Brian Whiteside)

A Life Worth Living (Booklet)

Becoming a Man of Influence (Booklet)

From Vision to Victory

Shadows: Book of Aleth, Part One

Revelation: Book of Aleth, Part Two

Shadow Remnant

Special Acknowledgements:

To my wonderful wife and children, I want to offer my deepest gratitude. You are my best and brightest partners as we walk the course of life together.

To my dear friends, you who believed in me when I needed it most, I want to say "thank you!"

To my church family who gives me such grace and the time it takes to write these books, I couldn't do this without you!

To all the Christian golfers out there, showing your faith and love for the Lord Jesus every time you step onto the fairway, thank you for walking the courses with me!

And, ultimately, I want to thank my Lord Jesus Christ who has called me into His service to build His kingdom for His glory. Amen.

Contents

Introduction

Enter the Clubhouse

NO MATTER WHAT you do, there is always that first thing that has to happen before the event can begin. Before a foundation is poured, the forms must be set. Before a painting is fashioned, the brushes must be prepped, and before you step out to play a round of golf, you have to enter the clubhouse. You've got to pay for the round, check in for your tee time and wait for the announcement of your name. You have to get through the introduction.

Yes, this is the introduction… the part of the book that most will skip over and head right into to the heart of the material. Have you ever tried to avoid the clubhouse and simply go to the first tee to begin your round? Skip the clubhouse and try to step onto the first tee without paying for the round and you may find yourself on the wrong end of the groundskeepers rake!

Just kidding…

However, I believe that you need a bit of an introduction to this book - this round of golf - an eighteen-hole journey as you walk the fairways with Jesus. That's what this book is all about.

There are beginnings to everything and the Christian life is no different. Jesus said, "If you abide in my word, you are truly my disciples, and you will know the truth, and the truth will set you free" (John 8:31-32). It's a simple truth, but to be a follower of Christ, you must first enter into that abiding relationship with Him.

There are those who have compared golf to life, and in some instances I believe that there is some validity to the comparison. Everyone will hit a bogey, make a mistake, find the rough or go out of bounds. In golf, as in life, there will be grand successes, great shots, miracle finishes and occasionally a cheering crowd. Every aspect of life will be found along the way, every emotion will find expression - from rich jubilation to stunning disappointment. But the one truth is always this: you'll never experience all that golf can provide if you never get on the course. And to get on the course, there's a payment to be made. And though I will talk a lot about golf in this book, you must remember that this book is about the Christian life.

Jesus said, "If anyone would come after me, let him deny himself and take up his cross daily and follow me" (Luke 9:23). To follow Jesus is to walk out onto the course of life in the steps of faith. That faith requires self-denial and a willingness to carry your cross.

So gear up, clean off your spikes, you've already paid for the round and can head off to chapter one – the first tee. Enjoy your round with the Lord Jesus Christ.

Hole One

The First Tee

I'VE PLAYED ON many golf courses. I've been the victim of some, the beneficiary of others. However, I've found that every course contains the same requirements: good shot making and course management. Okay, I also discovered one more thing, and it holds true for every course, that my favorite hole is always the first one.

There is nothing like stepping up to the first tee. An early morning tee-time brings a sense of renewal as the crisp air rushes through the lungs and the sound of a gentle breeze sings through the pine. Everything is fresh, new, and open on the first tee. The whole course stands before me, eighteen holes untouched by any of my mistakes. The first tee is the epitome of hopefulness.

Much the same way is the Christian life. When I came to know the Lord Jesus as Savior, it was a rush of excitement, a sense of destiny that awakened my heart to a new sense of hope and purpose. Consider Saul's (later taking the name Paul) experience in Acts 9:18, "And immediately something like scales fell from his eyes, and he regained his sight." That's what it was like for me. My eyes were opened to the world as if I had never seen it before. For the first time my mind and heart were open to the truth of God's word and I found hope. As a new Christian I stepped up to the first tee—the beginning of a spiritual journey filled with all the promises of God. Such hope! Such love! My whole life was made new in a moment and I was ready to take on the world.

Hope: The Reality of the First Tee

Very few golfers go to the first tee without a sense of hope. They step up to the tee box and, with a mighty swing, start a journey of eighteen holes that will bring them through the gauntlet of circumstances and emotions. But the first tee is the place of hope. With club in hand, the golfer steps up to the tee and says, "Today is the day I… break 80, beat the course record, hit every fairway, make every putt, etc." It doesn't matter if you're a weekend warrior or a tour professional, the first tee is hope.

Let me tell you, you can't even begin to experience a life filled with true hope until you surrender to Christ. At the end of this book, consider your life and destiny. Do you have the hope offered in Christ? Turn to the Bible, discover for yourself the person of Jesus, and realize that He came to give you everlasting life – hope for all time.

Hope is the wellspring of faith. Paul, in addressing the Colossian church, said as much. "We always thank God, the Father of our Lord Jesus Christ, when we pray for you, since we heard of your faith in Christ Jesus and of the love that you have for all the saints, because of the hope laid up for you in heaven. Of this you have heard before in the word of the truth, the gospel" (Colossians 1:3-5).

True faith cannot exist without hope. Faith will be examined more closely as we go on, but suffice it to say there is no such thing as faith without a real hope. Perhaps one of the most painful things to see is a Christian who, in contrast to their expressions of faith in Christ, possesses no hope.

But what is hope? For some, hope is little more than a positive affirmation of some wished for event or experience. That is, they don't have a solid reason to have hope, they just want something good and live in a wishing well. Real hope is more than just wishful thinking. Real hope is an expectation of a future experience that is anchored to a solid basis of belief.

Let me explain by example.

False hope, that is, wishful thinking, is a person playing the lottery. Here in Washington State (as with other states) you can pick a group of numbers and try to win a substantial amount of money. Whatever numbers you choose, you have no basis in fact that those particular numbers will actually be selected. There is no reason to believe that those numbers are guaranteed to fall into place according to your selection. That's false hope, wishful thinking with no real foundation.

True hope, hope that can be believed and counted on, is taking antibiotics to cure an infection. You receive the medicine from a reliable source, have confidence that the medicine will be effective to help fight the infection and know that others have had positive experiences with the medication prescribed. There is every reason to believe that the medicine will be effectual and you take the pill with hope – true hope.

Many people think that following Christ, being a Christian, is nothing more than a fantastical philosophy that has no basis for belief. However, if you examine the reality of Jesus Christ, you begin to see the facts. Jesus promised hope, and He proved it through His own resurrection. Multitudes of eyewitnesses testified to the fact that Jesus came back from the grave and ascended into heaven. All the aspects of the Messiah were fulfilled in Jesus. Not to belabor the point but you have received it from a reliable source (the Bible), you have confidence that it is effective (changed lives), and others have testified to you that it is true (two millennia of witnesses).

The first tee is the beginning of a journey along pristine fairways, lush greens, and fellow adventurers with a bag full of hope.

Where do you Tee Off?

On the first tee, and on every subsequent tee thereafter, a selection of color-coded markers defines the skill level of the tee box. The colors are, in order of difficulty from hardest to easiest: black, blue, white, yellow, red and silver. I've also seen green and orange tees. No matter, they all signify a state of expertise that a golfer has developed when they tee off. It is a troubling thing to see someone with a handicap a high as Bill Gates annual income try to tee off from the pro tees. Too many golfers frustrate themselves by trying to play from a more difficult position. As one club pro told me while I stood on the first tee: "Don't tee off harder than your enjoyment allows."

I remember when I was young (hopefully not that long ago) and my dad took me to the golf course. He wanted the experience to instill in me a desire for the game, a yearning to be on open fairways and long walks, but it didn't. In fact, it was many years later before I truly fell in love with the game.

Anyway, my dad took me to the first tee, a long par four that fell off (for my adolescent eyes) into a cliff the size of the Grand Canyon. He thrust a club in my hand and told me, "Now go and hit the ball." I stepped up to the tee box, looked at the small, round, green objects stabbed into the ground on either side of the tee box and decided that I liked the black ones. At my age, what did I know?

My dad heaved one of those "dad-sighs" that told me I made a tremendous blunder. He walked up to me, grabbed the club from my hands and demanded, "What were you thinking!" At that moment I was thinking about playing with my Hot Wheels™ back home—but I didn't tell him that. "Do you plan on playing from the pro tees when you've never been on a golf course?" He didn't, in fact, give me any time to answer because without hesitation he picked up my ball and parked it between the set of green orbs stabbed in the ground. "This is where you hit from."

In deference to my father, he was a remarkable golfer. Our house was littered with various trophies he won at some tournament or another. He loved the game, but insisted that it be played right. After I grew up my dad and I enjoyed many rounds together and his love of the game transferred into my own heart. In retrospect, however, I think it might have been wiser for him to give me some instruction before thrusting me onto the playing field. Ah, well, such is life.

And such is Christianity for some. Many have stepped up to the tee box of faith and decided then and there that they're going to play from the hardest position available. After all, if God has called them to play the game of life—why not start at the pro tees?

When I came forward in a church in California, publicly professing my faith in Christ Jesus and desire to worship and serve Him, the pastor presented me to the congregation and asked, quite loudly, "What are you going to do for the Lord?" What? What was I going to do for the Lord—I had no idea! I was saved on a Thursday and presented myself to the church that next Sunday and I was supposed to know what I would do for the Lord? Eighteen years of living and graduation from high school didn't give me a glimpse of what I would do for myself. Now, three days of knowing Jesus as my Savior, how could I begin to know what I would do for Him? Fortunately, the Lord moved me to another church with a pastor who gave me great grace and patience as I learned how to walk with Jesus.

Many Christians see their lives thrust to the "pro tees." They come to Jesus with such hope and joy they are eager to do anything, everything, for Him. A pastor or other church leader gravitates toward that enthusiasm and brings the new believer into some service or another. Yet, even Jesus gave His disciples three years of ministry and personal discipleship before they were sent out on their own. Paul says this in Philippians: "Let those of us who are mature think this way, and if in anything you think otherwise, God will reveal that also to you. Only let us hold true to what we have attained" (Philippians 3:15-16). Do you see? You cannot live up to what you haven't attained! Christianity is a growth prospect, and any new believer must be given the chance to grow.

Peter says, "But grow in the grace and knowledge of our Lord and Savior Jesus Christ. To him be the glory both now and to the day of eternity. Amen" (2 Peter 3:18). Again Peter says, "So put away all malice and all deceit and hypocrisy and envy and all slander. Like newborn infants, long for the pure spiritual milk, that by it you may grow up into salvation" (1 Peter 2:1-2). Hebrews 6:1 states, "Therefore let us leave the elementary doctrine of Christ and go on to maturity…" There is a process of spiritual growth that must take place long before a believer challenges the "pro tees."

When I started playing golf, seriously playing on a regular basis, my average score was triple digits. I was happy to just get it in the fairway. Now, however, my goal is less about making safe shots and more about making skilled ones. I see each hole for its opportunities for birdies and pars rather than bogies and doubles. That, however, didn't come without some practice, some effort and most of all, some experience.

For the Christian, teeing off from a position not suited to their subsequent maturity level is tantamount to disaster. I knew a man who demanded that he pastor a church. He was new in Christ, loved the Lord and wanted to serve Him, but he didn't want to take the time to discipline himself or pursue a process of growth that would provide him with the necessary maturity to handle that great responsibility. He thought he was acting on faith, tried to start a congregation on his own, and failed miserably when the pressure started mounting.

There are things that must be added to your faith before you venture into deeper waters. Hebrews says, "For everyone who lives on milk is unskilled in the word of righteousness, since he is a child. But solid food is for the mature, for those who have their powers of discernment trained by constant practice to distinguish good from evil" (Hebrews 5:13-14).

Peter states:

> For this very reason, make every effort to supplement your faith with virtue, and virtue with knowledge, and knowledge with self-control, and self-control with steadfastness, and steadfastness with godliness, and godliness with brotherly affection, and brotherly affection with love. For if these qualities are yours and are increasing, they keep you from being ineffective or unfruitful in the knowledge of our Lord Jesus Christ. ~ 2 Peter 1:5-8

There are things that must be added in order to make your life productive and effective. The discipline of the Christian life comes with faithful experience. As you navigate around the course and come back again, you learn, grow, and eventually are able to take on the more difficult levels— even making it to the spiritual "pros."

The first tee is that wonderful place where everything starts. If you're a golfer, you don't step up to the first tee without believing that the game is worth playing. Even if you're a hacker who plays golf with a weed eater in your bag, you still come! You don't have to play, you want to, and you want to because when you step up to the first tee you're hopeful, even excited about the next eighteen holes. Everything is right on the first tee.

Not only is the first tee the epitome of hope, it is also set up to provide a starting point suited to your level of expertise. Every first tee has multiple positions and you get to choose. You don't have to be as good as the pros to play; you can play according to your own skill level. Perhaps that is one of the things that make the game of golf so attractive.

In Christ, the wonder of that relationship with the Savior is the magnification of hope. Hope is the quintessential paradigm that is found in every believing heart. When you step up to the spiritual tee box and look out over the field of play that is set before you, that field called life, you find that there is an overwhelming sense of hopefulness. Not just the wishful thinking that accompanies despair, but a true sense of hope that is anchored to promises more secure than anything this world can offer. A hope that is set in Heaven, bound by cords of love, and provided by the Savior.

And the new believer has a place to tee off! You don't have to wait until you're perfect to begin because God has provided a place for the novice as well. But you don't remain a novice. If you follow Jesus, walking by faith in accordance with His word, you will discover that your "skills" will grow—your faith and love. As Paul said to the Philippians:

> Not that I have already obtained this or am already perfect, but I press on to make it my own, because Christ Jesus has made me his own.
> 13 Brothers, I do not consider that I have made it my own. But one thing I do: forgetting what lies behind and straining forward to what lies ahead,
> 14 I press on toward the goal for the prize of the upward call of God in Christ Jesus. ~ Philippians 3:12-14

Have you stepped up to the first tee? Have you trusted in Christ Jesus as your Savior and Lord? Have you entered through the "narrow gate" (Matthew 7:13)?

It is the launch of a journey that will end in glory, a starting point of a new life that breaks upon your soul like the early morning sun cresting the horizon in brilliant splendor. The first tee is where it all begins.

Hole Two

The Fairway

I REMEMBER MY longest drive. With the sound like an explosion off the face of the club, the ball soared through the air like a missile. Two hundred yards, two hundred and fifty and still it was in the air. It landed and bounded forward like a rabbit from a hole. It bounced again, rolled, and finally came to rest, three hundred and fifty three yards from the tee box.

Okay, for the purpose of full disclosure, I will admit that the fairway was extremely downhill, the ground was hard as concrete, and there was a bit of a breeze blowing from behind me… what did I care, the shot felt fantastic. There it was: my

ball in the fairway and only a chip shot away from the green. (I'll tell you about the rest of the hole later.)
Being in the fairway does not guarantee a successful round of golf, but not being in the fairway almost always guarantees a bad one. In fact, one of the realities that I always seem to encounter is the simple truth that the fairway is not always fair. This came to light when I stepped up to the tenth tee and pondered the obstacle that stood before me.

Like a sentinel, a guardian to prevent any and all who dared to attack the green, stood the widest, tallest tree on the entire golf course. This wooden monstrosity didn't stand off to the side like some aloof, unconcerned sentry. Nor did it protect the green from a vantage point beyond my (or anyone else's) range. It stood, mocking and laughing in the breeze, waving its leafy arms right in the center of the fairway.

What was I to do? Give up… no, giving up is never the option. Should I yield to the will of the crazed golf course architect that decided to leave a tree smack-dab in the middle of the fairway and hit around the tree, insuring nothing better than a par? Well, that was not an option either. I might have shaken my fist at the heavens for the audacity of growing a perfectly fine tree in a perfectly awful location. But that wouldn't do. You see, obstacles are always around and God allows them for the testing and improvement of our faith.

The Fairway isn't Always Fair

Every child in the world has heard these words from their parents: "Life isn't always fair." Growing up, my dad used that statement as a mantra. Occasionally it involved one of the children receiving a gift or treat and not the others. More often than not it revolved around one of the children getting in trouble and the other's escaping discipline. But, from a perspective here in the world, the refrain certainly seems to hold true that life isn't always fair.

As I stood, gazing at the massive obstacle before me (the tree), I complained much like many others, "That's not fair." However, my golfing partner stepped to the tee-box, hit his drive over the top branches, and reached the fairway just beyond. With a glint in his eye and a sly smile, he said, "it's not that bad." Sure, for him it's not that bad at all. But, he was more accurate with his driver and all I could see was a wall of leaves and branches.

God doesn't always seem fair either. This reality strikes the life of every believer in Christ and the first place that God seems unfair is when it comes to people.

Have you ever told God that others seem to prosper, that others who do not have the same dedication as you seem to thrive? Have you ever said to God, "It's not fair?" You're not alone. Hear the words of Jeremiah, "Righteous are you, O Lord, when I complain to you; yet I would plead my case before you. Why does the way of the wicked prosper? Why do all who are treacherous thrive?" (Jeremiah 12:1).

I know that I have challenged God in the same way. There have been times when I questioned God about His fairness, when I watched others succeed with lavish abundance and I seemed to troll about in the basement of God's blessings. I have felt the same as the psalmist who wrote: "For I was envious of the arrogant when I saw the prosperity of the wicked" (Psalm 73:3). At a glance it appears that God is not fair, that God allows the wicked to prosper when it should be the faithful. However, you must never trust anything you only see at a glance.

The challenge for the Christian is to believe God over observation. Just because you see a wicked person prosper does not mean that you see the entire picture. In a world free from sin there would never be a "Paul" in prison and a "Caesar" on the throne. The righteous would thrive and wickedness would be gone. It might surprise you, but we don't live in a world free from sin.

You might say then, as some have said, that if God is all that the Bible says He is then why doesn't He step in, cast down the wicked and uphold the righteous. He will. That time is coming, and it is coming faster than any of us might surmise. However, God is also patient and not wanting anyone to perish but all come to repentance (2 Peter 3:9). God will hold all men accountable. Just because you cannot see the full measure of God's wrath on the wicked only means that you cannot see the full picture.

The fairness of God toward people is one thing, but is God fair when it comes to circumstances? How often do you experience some obstacle or difficulty in life that brings you up short and then question the fairness of God? It happens to everyone.

On one particularly bright afternoon Chuck and I played a round of golf at Osan Airbase in Korea. The hours passed and finally we teed off on the eighteenth hole. My shot, a bit of a slice, started to the left of the fairway then drifted to the right. I was in the rough, but not too bad. Then it was Chuck's turn. He hit a beauty, an arrow shot right down the center of the fairway. Then the strangest event occurred. As if struck by a baseball bat, the ball hit the ground and ricocheted at a ninety-degree angle right into a small pond.

We both were startled and quite surprised at the strange bounce of his golf ball. With bags in tow, we walked down the hill until we came to the place where his ball hit. It was a sprinkler head, ever so slightly lifted up from the grass. The ball hit on the edge of the sprinkler and ricocheted into its watery grave. Silent, we stood shaking our heads at the incredible misfortune. That day Chuck had suffered a difficult round of golf and his tee shot on the eighteenth hole was his best—until that infamous sprinkler head. He wanted to curse the groundskeeper; he wanted to pound that sprinkler into dust. However, he remained composed and just said… you guessed it… "It's not fair."

This is, perhaps, the most difficult area of debate when it comes to the issue of God's fairness. Some disconnect God from any negative circumstance, as if God is aloof and unresponsive to the travails of life. Others accuse God of wrong-doing when times get tough, as if God is some mean-spirited Deity that takes pleasure in watching people move like rats through a maze. I won't try to belabor the issue of the sovereignty of God. Suffice it to say, God is sovereign. If there is anything outside of God's sovereign influence, if anything can happen where God does not have absolute authority, then God cannot be God because there is something that exists outside of His will. I rejoice, however, in knowing that there is nothing outside of His will.

The Apostle Paul was a man who faced circumstances that carried him through such tragic hardship that most people would have given up in despair. Consider what Paul had to say:

> I know how to be brought low, and I know how to abound. In any and every circumstance, I have learned the secret of facing plenty and hunger, abundance and need. I can do all things through him who strengthens me. ~ Philippians 4:12-13

The idea conveyed in the statement "learned the secret" can mean that he was "initiated into the secret." Circumstances are God's initiation process to train all Christians to be content—not in circumstances but in Him. Too many Christians want to be content in their circumstances and when they don't find contentment they blame God for being "unfair." You must find your contentment in Christ alone and allow Him to be the ruler of all your circumstances—no matter what they are.

The problem with the issue of fairness is that it is completely subjective, given over to the mind of the viewer. What I consider fair, you might not consider fair. What I think is acceptable to life you might think is absolutely annoying. The reason for this disparity is that we share different points of view. Now think about this: God also has a point of view. He can see the end from the beginning; He knows the future as well as the past; He comprehends the outcome long before we ever arrive there. So, when difficult times are allowed to process through your life and you cannot understand what is happening, take heart that God does know and He has permitted this for your spiritual growth.

Remember what Jesus said: "I have said these things to you, that in me you may have peace. In the world you will have tribulation. But take heart; I have overcome the world" (John 16:33). Peace for the Christian is not found in anything other than harmony with Jesus. Circumstances will rise and fall in their various challenges but the believer must always face them with faith in Christ. Otherwise, if you try and find your peace from the shifting world around you, invariably you will cry foul and tell God that He's just not fair.

The Fairway is the Best Place to Play

For all the challenges that course designers engineer, the fairway is still the best place to play. This may seem like an obvious thing, but how many times have you tried to "cut the corner" and then put your golf ball right in the lake? Very few golfers can take shortcuts on the golf course and come away victorious.

I stepped up to the tee, driver in hand and the green just under three hundred yards away. A dog-leg to the left stood before me with tall evergreen trees lining both sides of the fairway. I played with two other men who were complete strangers to me (I'd say perfect strangers, but nobody's perfect). They had played the course often. It was my first time.

"Don't try to cut the dog-leg," the older man said. "The trees might look easy, but nobody makes it around the corner. Just hit it in the fairway and play it from there."

Did I take the advice? Of course... you know the answer... in no way did I listen. I took my driver and hit a brilliant shot. On a line over the trees my ball sailed with maximum determination to cut the corner. I thought I had made it. The older man just shook his head.

I walked in the direction of my ball flight, anxious to see it resting on the green or somewhere nearby. I looked, I searched, and I strained my eyes to find that little white orb to no avail. What I didn't know was that the older man waited behind me in the trees.

"Hey there," he shouted, "is this your ball?"

I turned and went to the place where the man stood. I hung my head with despair and embarrassment. My ball was nestled against the trunk of a large pine. I should have listened.

You see, the fairway is not necessarily meant to be easy, it's meant to be playable. Not every fairway is the same. They all have different challenges and difficulties, different skills are required to play them well and different knowledge is necessary. The more often you play a particular course, the more familiar you become with the nuances of each fairway and the more potential you have to make good decisions and play well.

To the casual observer God doesn't always seem fair, but there is only one way to live. You must choose to live for Christ and then play the life God has given you along the course that He has designed. And consider this: the more often you play the course of God's design, the more familiar you become with it and the better you will be able to play.

But what is God's fairway? Though I will cover this more in later chapters, the simple answer is: God's fairway is His word. He has given us His word in order to know the way for life. Consider what was commanded to the Israelites. "You shall walk in all the way that the Lord your God has commanded you, that you may live, and that it may go well with you, and that you may live long in the land that you shall possess." (Deuteronomy 5:33). Again, in Deuteronomy 10:12, "And now, Israel, what does the Lord your God require of you, but to fear the Lord your God, to walk in all his ways, to love him, to serve the Lord your God with all your heart and with all your soul."

This same thought is carried on in Isaiah. "And a highway shall be there, and it shall be called the Way of Holiness; the unclean shall not pass over it. It shall belong to those who walk on the way; even if they are fools, they shall not go astray" (Isaiah 35:8). Deviation from God's way is simply disastrous. Shortcuts, trying to make your own way, trying to find your own path rather than following the Master Designer's plan will only put your life into hazards and situations that you must then recover from. Paul encourages the church with these words:

> Not that I have already obtained this or am already perfect, but I press on to make it my own, because Christ Jesus has made me his own. Brothers, I do not consider that I have made it my own. But one thing I do: forgetting what lies behind and straining forward to what lies ahead, I press on toward the goal for the prize of the upward call of God in Christ Jesus. ~ Philippians 3:12-14

There is only one way to go—the way heavenward—the way of Christ.

You should never let your perception of fairness discolor your view of God and His dealings in your life. As you strive along, working your way to try and make it through life, there are challenges and difficulties that always rise up. Even if you've "kept it in the fairway" you will still find that your experiences seem unfair at times.

Remember that 353 yard drive? When I got to the ball it sat in an old divot, resting against the leading edge of the mark. I was in the fairway, but still faced a challenge to get the ball up and down. But, like James says, "…for you know that the testing of your faith produces steadfastness" (James 1:3).

I came home on leave from the Air Force one summer and went golfing with my dad. Though he couldn't hit the ball very far (an average drive of about 250 yards) he was one of those men who never missed the fairway. Anyway, we were on the last par-three hole and he wanted to raise the stakes. Whoever came closest to the pin, the other had to buy lunch. I had never beaten my dad at anything but on this day I was making better shots and had the advantage. So, with arrogance, I took the bet.

I turned my back for just a moment when my dad hit his ball. My turn came and I played a straight shot, thirty feet from the pin. However, I didn't see my dad's ball anywhere. I was sure he was off the green.
We walked around the green and he feigned irritation. I looked through the rough, in the traps, and out of bounds, but there was no sign of his shot.

Casually my dad said, "Son, why not try looking in the hole."

There it was, resting comfortably against the pin at the bottom of the cup—it's just not fair.

Hole Three

The Rough

AN EARLY MORNING tee-time brought me to the course. Dew dressed the ground and shimmered in the rising sun. Spider webs hung lazily on tree branches, dripping with moisture. Tall pines gently stood against a blue sky. It was one of those mornings when you saw every detail in splendid relief. Birds chirped a welcome to the outfitted warriors who slipped on spiked shoes and swung their clubs to warm up.

I ventured to the first tee, partnered with a man who may have golfed with Moses. He had an ancient collection of seven clubs carried in a tan, leather bag. Stooped and slow, I let him tee off first. Though he did have a persimmon driver in his bag, he took his seven iron and hit it about 150 yards down the fairway. I hit and then we walked up to his ball. With his seven iron, again, he hit it about 150 yards in the fairway. A chip and a putt and he made par.

That was his game: seven iron, fairway; seven iron, fairway; chip and a putt. If it was a par five, he just hit another seven iron shot. He didn't score any birdies, but he never missed the fairway and it was, literally, par for the course. I didn't have as much success that day.

Even off the first tee I struck a banana shot into the right rough. The third hole was worse, a shot into the right rough that careened off a tree and into a ditch. Hole after hole I played from either the right or left rough. In fact, I think I only played from the fairway four times the entire round. My score was awful, and my attitude was little better.
As we walked off the eighteenth hole, me with a bogey and my seasoned companion with… you guessed it… a par, he gave me a slight chuckle.

"Young man," he said slyly, "you'll never play a good round of golf if you always play from the rough."

I just nodded. I outdrove him on every hole, but he played such a disciplined round of golf that it almost looked tedious. Yet the results were there; his round was nearly flawless and mine straggled all over the course. How true it is: you cannot play a good round from the rough.

Mistakes Leave You in the Rough

No one wants to enter the rough. You play from the rough because of some error. There are times when I've played a good round of golf and avoided the rough, but eventually everyone will have to find their way through the tall grasses and thick clumps of turf that make up a major portion of any golf course. Think of how the Apostle Paul describes it: "For I do not do the good I want, but the evil I do not want is what I keep on doing" (Romans 7:19).

Those errors, those shots that leave you in the rough, are known in the Bible as sins. We will cover this issue in greater detail in a later chapter, but suffice it to say, sin is the disconnect of the human experience from the right ways of God. You must understand that all of humanity has lost touch, strayed and sinned against a holy God. The hope of life is this: Jesus is our Great Redeemer. He alone has done what no one else could. He purchased all humanity with His death on the cross and provided hope to all who believe.

Yet there are times when even Christians make errors, sometimes grievous errors that send life into a tailspin of sin. Imagine it like this. Every Christian is in the kingdom of God by invitation – through the death and resurrection of Jesus. Just like there are only select golfers who have the privilege to play in what is known as an "invitational" so it is for all who respond to God's invitation to faith in Christ. Now, just because a pro golfer is playing in an invitational does not mean they make no mistakes and never enter the rough. They still do. 1 John 1:8 says, "If we say we have no sin, we deceive ourselves, and the truth is not in us." So, just as all golfers enter the rough so all Christians will suffer the difficulties of sin—of missing God's fairway and having to deal with the challenge of the rough.

Yet the rough lines the fairways and that seems a bit unfair. A bit of a slice, a little more hook than you hoped and you find yourself in trouble. It reminds me of what God said to Joshua, "Only be strong and very courageous, being careful to do according to all the law that Moses my servant commanded you. Do not turn from it to the right hand or to the left, that you may have good success wherever you go" (Joshua 1:7). Joshua gave this same instruction to the people of Israel in Joshua 23:6. If you know your Biblical history, you know that it didn't take long for the entire nation to turn aside.

Once you stray to the "left or right" you find yourself in a world of difficulty that forces choices not normally associated with the way you hoped things would go. Even as I write this chapter, I am inundated with memories of problems that occurred in my life due to my poor choices. In fact, there was a time when I thought that no opportunity to recover existed—I was deep in the rough.

I nearly gave up. I looked out over the trouble that I found myself in and thought that there was no rescue, no hope and no one who could understand the challenge that I faced. My whole life appeared to be nearly shipwrecked on a single moment. I still had my faith and my family, but I saw no future. So I prayed.

I played a round of golf on a course that was thick with rough on every hole. I spent a moment in a patch of rough that bore reminders of the nightmarish grasses of the U.S. Open. I stood in knee-deep thatch and, after several minutes of a painstaking search, I found my ball. It had settled to the ground, surrounded by a hoard of long, wispy strands that guarded it as if my ball was the Hope Diamond.

There are consequences to hitting in the rough and a cost for escaping the wayward shot.

Escaping the Rough

"Sometimes you just have to take your medicine," say many golfers who happen to slice or hook their ball into a patch of trouble. But what does that mean? It means the trouble you're in might require a shot simply to get back into play. To try and make the "perfect shot" or to pretend that you're not in trouble will only serve to aggravate the situation further.

Remember that "patch of rough" I told you about earlier. The thatch was deep, nearly up to my knees, and the ball had nestled to the ground. The green was reachable, about 140 yards, if I had a sensible lie. I could have tried to make the green—but a water hazard stood between me and the "perfect shot." I could have picked up my ball in frustration and left the course. There was really only one thing to do: I hacked it out into the fairway and continued. I shot a bogey on that hole, but the damage might have been more severe if I tried the ultimate gamble.

The idea that a Christian never has trouble, makes no mistakes and enjoys the constant, sweet favor of God is a myth. Bad choices happen, sins are committed and the hand of God reaches down to discipline and chastise His children. Everyone slices into the rough now and again. The question is: what to do. Well, there is hope. Just as a person has to make certain decisions to escape the rough, so Christians have decisions to make to escape the trouble that comes with sin.

Remember: **H.O.P.E.**

First, you must *humble* yourself before the Lord.

Humility is the key. If you hold onto pride and self-importance, you will never be able to see clearly to deal with sin. Pride does not own up to mistakes.

Consider what took place in the garden of God—that place called Eden. God confronted Adam with his sin. Genesis 3:11, "Who told you that you were naked? Have you eaten of the tree of which I commanded you not to eat?" Did Adam respond, "You're right, Lord?" Did Adam own up to his sin? No. Adam replied, ""The woman whom you gave to be with me, she gave me fruit of the tree, and I ate" (Genesis 3:12). Adam puts the blame at the feet of his wife, and more than that, he almost blames God because he said it was "the woman you put here with me." Almost as if Adam wanted to say, "God, if it wasn't for that woman this would never have happened. You should never have given her to me—look what she did!"

But humility will own up to sin. When a man can humble himself before others, and especially before God, he will recognize the truth of his own life and be willing to do those things that bring restoration. Consider what proverbs says, "When pride comes, then comes disgrace, but with the humble is wisdom" (Proverbs 11:2). Think of the humility of David. He had committed adultery and murder and in his arrogance thought he could cover up the sin. God confronts him through the prophet Nathan and David repents. Look at his words in Psalm 51, "For I know my transgressions, and my sin is ever before me" (v. 3). You can repent of sin only when you can face the reality of sin—and that takes humility.

Second, you must *objectively* look at the trouble.

I went golfing with a man who constantly sliced his shots into the rough. On the tee, in the rough (or the trees) was his pattern. By the time we reached the fifth hole his attitude was so gloomy it drained the enjoyment completely out of the game. He knew his trouble, he humbly acknowledged his error, but all he did was immerse himself in despair. I finally asked him, "Have you ever considered aiming to the left?" As if that was the greatest revelation since the invention of the light bulb, he made the change and actually hit a few fairways.

It's time to put the pity-party away. For the Christian, there is no reason to remain in subjective despair, to linger in the dungeons of doubt and self-loathing. If you know you've done wrong, if you know you've sinned against God, own up to it and realize that God has provided the means of restoration. Get up; cry out to the Lord who is compassionate and willing to save.

Perhaps you've felt like David when he prayed, "For evils have encompassed me beyond number; my iniquities have overtaken me, and I cannot see; they are more than the hairs of my head; my heart fails me" (Psalm 40:12). Then you need to have the same focus as David, "Be pleased, O Lord, to deliver me! O Lord, make haste to help me!" (Psalm 40:13).

Third, you must *plan* your next move correctly.

The choices for a golfer who ends up in trouble might be many or they might be few. I've been in the rough and the shot was simple, an easy choice to make. I've been in rough where the only option was to chip out into the fairway and try again. Sometimes it's so bad that you can't even find your ball and must re-tee and start over. But you must plan your next move correctly.

I hit a drive that ended up on the edge of a pond. The ball was just an inch below the surface of the water and I remember watching a pro golfer (I can't remember who) hit a shot just like mine and do so with great success. Therefore, I rolled up my pants, took off my socks and shoes, and proceeded to slap at the water with my club. It was the wettest, worst decision I made on a golf course—ever. And there, just below the surface of the water, sat my ball. I didn't plan my shot very well.

There is only one move appropriate for a person in sin: repent. If you've humbled yourself before the Lord, if you have left behind the pity-party and looked at your situation with objectivity, then you need to make the decision to turn around and leave your sin behind. Paul said in Acts 26:20, "...but declared first to those in Damascus, then in Jerusalem and throughout all the region of Judea, and also to the Gentiles, that they should repent and turn to God, performing deeds in keeping with their repentance."

There are three things you must see from this text, they are: repent, return, and respond. All three are choices that you must make in order to move beyond the trouble. Repent: choose to turn away from sin. Return to God: make the choice to set your path squarely in God's word (we'll discuss this in detail in a later chapter). Respond in obedience: take the necessary steps to live out the faith that God has given you. This might mean that you have to recompense those you hurt, to face the legal consequences if your sin was also a crime, or to seek the forgiveness of others. But make the necessary plans to start walking away from sin and into the path of Christ.

Fourth, you must *execute* the plan faithfully.

The reason many Christians don't find freedom from sin is simple—they don't execute the steps necessary to change. Luke 3:10, as the crowds gathered around John the Baptist they asked, "What then shall we do?" John tells them. With each inquiry, John the Baptist gives them the necessary evidence of a changed life. What John could not do is to execute it for them

The rich ruler ended up in that same situation. "Teacher, what good deed must I do to have eternal life?" (Matthew 19:16). That's a good question! Jesus told him. Jesus gave that man a chance to take the necessary steps to leave behind his self-involved life and follow the Savior. What happened? "When the young man heard this he went away sorrowful, for he had great possessions" (Matthew 19:22). That young man would not make the choice to execute the plan laid out before him by Christ.

I love to watch the pro's play. It is amazing to watch them stand in the rough, trees in the way, sand and water all around and they make some amazing shot to get themselves back into play. They didn't want to be in the rough, but once there they don't lament and pout. They walk up to their ball, explore the terrain, examine the possibilities, talk with their caddy and finally execute a plan of action that provides them the best possible chance. It's the only way to play golf—you have to take the next shot.

Let me ask you this question: are you in a sin that is bearing down upon your heart? You're not alone. Remember, 1 John 1:8 says, "If we say we have no sin, we deceive ourselves, and the truth is not in us." The question is: do you want to leave your sin behind? Do you want to escape the rough and put your life right with God? Then humble yourself, look at the sin objectively, plan your steps in accordance with God's word and then execute that plan.

These steps will give you: H.O.P.E.

Hole Four

The Green

IT WAS A beautiful spring morning. I headed to the golf course early and the first tee was wide open. Dew nestled on the green fairway. The sun sent ribbons of light waving through tree branches and illumined a soft mist that lazily drifted through the surrounding woods. The fresh scent of pine hung in the air and all the elements of the world seemed to converge on this moment with breathtaking serenity.

I pulled my driver from the bag, the rattle of clubs momentarily disturbing the tranquil silence. I placed my ball on the tee, tightened my glove ever so slightly, and after a couple of practice swings let loose a powerful shot down the lush fairway. I approached my ball, now only two hundred yards from the green, set my feet and swung my four-iron. Away it went, lifted off the earth with the trajectory of an arrow and the gentleness of a feather. It landed on the green, no more than twenty feet from the hole—a par five in two.

Two putts for a birdie. Perhaps I'd even get an eagle! My round was off to a good start as I set my clubs near the green and retrieved my putter. I stepped onto the green. The break was left-to-right, uphill and with a bit of a ridge to contend with. One putt, no problem—still a birdie chance. Putt two and the ball lips out of the hole. Putt three—it comes to rest just millimeters from the cup. I four putted a bogey.

Everyone loves to hit the long-ball. A well placed approach shot is a thing to behold. Precision around the edges, with a ball chipped within inches of the cup is a thrill. However, and with deference to all the great shots that are made, I find that how I play the green will make or break my round. There are fine details on the green that most amateur, weekend-warrior golfers miss. Occasionally these fine details will even make or break a professional golfer's round and might even snatch defeat out of the hand of victory.

Some of these details, like the contour of the green, the speed, even the direction the grass is growing will have an effect on the way your ball will roll. Why did the ball roll to a millimeter from the cup? Could it be that the grain (the direction the grass is growing) is away from the hole? Why did the ball lip out around the rim of the cup? Could it be that, at just the last moment, the contour took the ball from a true line and diverted it just enough to miss? These details will always play into the round and change a would-be eagle putt into four-putt bogey.

There's a funny thing about the details of life—they don't ever seem to go away. No matter how much we take care of the "big picture" you cannot avoid the reality that it might be the small, seemingly insignificant things that disrupt life more than anything else. This is true in everything. My wife and I moved into a brand new modular home and, after months of quiet enjoyment in our new abode, we smelled smoke from the kitchen. I scoured the kitchen with my eyes, looking for anything that might be on fire. Then I noticed something strange. Behind the microwave, the power outlet was scarred with brown and black marks, almost like burn marks. What was the problem? I shut off the power to the outlet, took it apart and found my problem. The wires on the inside of the outlet were not tightened down. That little detail could have burned our home to ashes.

Pay Attention to Details

Have you ever observed how God pays attention to details? Consider this statement: "Are not two sparrows sold for a penny? And not one of them will fall to the ground apart from your Father. But even the hairs of your head are all numbered." (Matthew 10:29-30). Imagine that! The God who created the universe, the King of kings and Lord of lords, the Savior and Sustainer of life is so detail minded that He even has the hairs of your head counted. Think about it. The phrase, "Don't sweat the small stuff" has become a proverbial axiom in our culture. But do Christians need to concern themselves over the details?

I talked with a club pro at a small course in the middle of nowhere. He mentioned that too many weekend golfers practice the wrong skills. He said that they work over eighty percent of the time on their driver and less than five on their putter. However, he said, over half the game is played on the green and less than twenty-five percent of the game is played with a driver.

I think life actually demands an attention to detail that many are unwilling to give. Yet successful people across the ages have this in common: they consider the small things. James tells us this: "Look at the ships also: though they are so large and are driven by strong winds, they are guided by a very small rudder wherever the will of the pilot directs. So also the tongue is a small member, yet it boasts of great things. How great a forest is set ablaze by such a small fire" (James 3:4-5). And though James is directly referring to the issue of what we say and how we speak, I think the illustration carries us to understand that there is a reality that the little things (such as rudders and tongues) actually can make the biggest difference.

The Game is Won or Lost on the Green

You're never done with a round of golf until the final putt. Nowhere was this more evident than in the final round of the 2008 U.S. Open when Tiger Woods sank the final putt to send the Open to a playoff match with Rocco Mediate. The crowd burst into hysteria and Rocco stood nodding his head in knowing appreciation of what just happened.

You may have experienced something along these same lines. I know I have. No, not in such a theatre as the U.S. Open, but during a local competition with other pastors while I enjoyed some time at a retreat. It was the final hole of the just-for-fun tournament. Mind you, I am a fairly competitive man by nature and there on the eighteenth green I stood over a fifteen foot birdie putt that would put me one shot under my competitors. I stepped up to the ball and the world felt like it moved in slow motion. The only gallery I had was the three other men on the green and the meandering pastors who had already finished their rounds. The waning sun cast long shadows across the grass and a warm breath of wind wafted through the trees. I stepped up to the ball. Took a deep breath to calm my nerves… and with one smooth swing watched my ball track right along the line and into the hole. It was a birdie putt to win by one stroke – and I did it! The other pastors' simple congratulations echoed in my ears like thunderous applause as I removed my ball from the cup. Ah… sweet victory!

Many great approach shots have been foiled by faulty putting. And many horrendous experiences along the fairway have been rescued by a great touch on the green. You see, you may have faltered along the way, stumbled up the fairways of life and ended up in the rough through poor and sinful decisions. But it is possible to rescue this, your "round" called life. You see, the green is the target – the objective – and though it may have cost you hardship and heartache along the way, you can still make the most of the moment that you have and recover from your bad shots. I am always amazed at how one good putt can amend for a myriad of difficulties that it took to get there.

One of the great images of a rescued life is the Apostle Paul. Here it is from his own words: "Though formerly I was a blasphemer, persecutor, and insolent opponent. But I received mercy because I had acted ignorantly in unbelief" (1 Timothy 1:13). As he wrote to his young charge, Timothy, he remembered the failure of his life along the way: a violent, blaspheming persecutor. He echoes this same sentiment to the church at Corinth, "For I am the least of the apostles, unworthy to be called an apostle, because I persecuted the church of God" (1 Corinthians 15:9). Yet, look at his follow-up statement in verse 10, "But by the grace of God I am what I am."

That is you and I. Faltering, failing and finding ourselves off target. But, God's grace is there, you can still get it together and find your life restored in Christ. You may have to "take a drop" but the green is still waiting, the objective of your life from God's point of view is still there. And, when you get there, take a deep breath and know that victory can be won if you don't give up.

As the Apostle Paul looked back on his "round," he finished victoriously:

> I have fought the good fight, I have finished the race, I have kept the faith. 8 Henceforth there is

> laid up for me the crown of righteousness, which the Lord, the righteous judge, will award to me on that Day, and not only to me but also to all who have loved his appearing. ~ 2 Timothy 4:7-8

The Green Takes Precision and Patience

I've already lamented on how I turned a potential eagle into a bogey, but that experience is a great example of what is needed on the green - and the "greens" of life: precision and patience. In that previous experience, the level of excitement I possessed actually possessed me. I had hit a marvelous second shot and I stood upon the green with adrenalin rushing through my veins. I wanted to sink the putt quickly, and rushed through my routine only to miss the first try. That sent me to a greater state of agitation and I missed the second putt as it lipped out, only to be two feet away. I dribbled the third putt so close that a breeze might have pushed it in. Then finally, with a huff, I tapped it in.

I learned a valuable lesson that day, and so should all of us who rush through our lives. The Christian life (like golf) demands precision and patience. In 1 Corinthians 9:26 there is a marvelous illustration that shines a light on this truth: "So I do not run aimlessly; I do not box as one beating the air."

Let your imagination loose for just a moment. Think of a man who is running "aimlessly." There he goes! Not knowing where he's headed and in a desperate hurry to get there. What about a man "beating the air?" Picture in your mind a boxer in the ring with his opponent, swinging wildly at nothing in particular. The "running" man goes nowhere fast and the "beating" man hits nothing in particular. So it is with those who lack precision.

Those illustrations give a clear view of what it looks like to live without precision. Ecclesiastes clarifies this, "If the iron is blunt, and one does not sharpen the edge, he must use more strength, but wisdom helps one to succeed" (Ecclesiastes 10:10). Why do professional golfers practice putting over and over… and over again? Because to read the green, know the contours, understand the grain of the grass, hit it with the right touch and get the ball into the hole requires precision. Such wisdom brings success.

I'll be honest and confess… I play a quick round of golf. I take long strides up the fairway, step up to strike the ball without much deliberation and evaluate the greens with undo haste. It is possible to get away with speed off the tee, with rapid walking along the fairway, but when it comes to the green it demands a slower pace and a patient disposition. Patience is, without over-stressing it, perhaps the greatest asset on the green.

But what about life?

People rush through life as if there is a drive to get to the end of it as quickly as possible. I remember as a child, it seemed that time moved so slowly. It was sluggish, even ponderous, at times. It took "forever" to get to Christmas or to make it to summer vacations. But, as I have matured and circumnavigated the sun these past many years, time has a tendency now to move at a much more rapid pace. Though I doubt the planet is moving around the sun any faster or that it's spinning at greater velocity, life is more on the move now than it's ever been. Yet (and I say this with all deference to the adage), the best things in life take time.

The words of James 5:7 come to mind: "Be patient, therefore, brothers, until the coming of the Lord. See how the farmer waits for the precious fruit of the earth, being patient about it, until it receives the early and the late rains." The context of this passage is the patience needed to wait upon the Lord's return – especially in the face of suffering. But, the illustration is apropos.

Having lived on a farm for some part of my childhood, I watched my dad work the fields with such resolve, with more grit than the dirt he plowed, with a steeled determination to get the land ready to receive the crop. As if from his own sheer willpower the wheat harvest would rise from the earth. But once the crop was planted he had to wait. And wait. And wait! Rains would come and go. Sunshine would fall upon the hills. And then, like a fresh blanket upon the earth, the land was covered in new, green growth. The weeks passed and soon the lush green growth transformed into amber waves of grain. And his patience paid off – the harvest time had come.

And, like needing patience on the green, it takes patience in life. The Christian life is not a sprint it is a marathon and God's work in your life is not like microwave popcorn – more like a slow-cooker. As Paul says in Philippians 1:6, "And I am sure of this, that he who began a good work in you will bring it to completion at the day of Jesus Christ." If you've ever heard anybody say: "God's not finished with me yet," they're telling the truth. None of us are completely perfect but all of us who walk with Christ are on the right road.

Remember, the game is won or lost on the green. Don't be in a hurry to just get through the moment, but be patient and precise. Consider the details. Step onto the green of your life and make sure you take a moment to pay attention. Slow down long enough to know what the situation is. And put yourself in the best position for success.

Hole Five

The Fringe

I LOOKED UP from my tee shot on a clouded and drizzly day. The green sat nearly two hundred yards away on the first par three of the front nine. The air was heavy with the chill of late autumn and many of the trees had already given up their leaves, blanketing the ground with a colorful assortment of gold and crimson.

I sized up my shot, stepped to the ball and… thwack! The ball tracked through the air like a missile, straight and true toward the green. The elevated green was hidden from sight, but I knew that my four-iron was sufficient to carry the bunkers in front of the green and go the distance. My friend hit his ball and, as was his difficulty all day, missed his shot to the right. No worries, it was a joyful time to be out on the course. We retrieved our bags and trekked up the hill to make our next shot.

My friend found his ball short of the green to the right and nestled in thick patch of grass just in front of a small dogwood. With no shot available he took a drop and the ensuing penalty stroke, and then hit his ball onto the green. As competitive as I am, though he was my good friend, I smiled a bit, thinking that I had reached the green and would gain another stroke on him. Two putts for a par - maybe one for a birdie! I walked the remaining distance up the hill to the green only to discover I fell short… I was on the fringe.

A Place of Transition

What is the "fringe?" It is a small belt of well-cut grass which encircles the green yet is similar in condition to the fairway. It is that place of transition from fairway to green.

Everyone goes through periods of transition, moving from potential to probable. That's what the fringe is - the place between potential and probable. The Christian life is filled with periods of transition and is only experienced by those who are willing to take all the potential of their lives and do more than they have done before - but it takes a willingness to go through those transitional stages.

Paul makes this clear when he declares that all those who are in Christ are in a state of continual growth, transitioning from glory to glory: "And we all, with unveiled face, beholding the glory of the Lord, are being transformed into the same image from one degree of glory to another. For this comes from the Lord who is the Spirit." (2 Corinthians 3:18).

But why can't Jesus just leave me the way I am? I've heard that question many times, from a variety of people in every walk and venue of life. They're happy with their own condition and don't have any problem with their own self-satisfaction. It's like playing golf with those who have no desire to improve their game, no hunger to get better, no drive to set a higher bar than that which they have already set. They don't mind shooting 130 in a round. And when they are told to make a few adjustments by those who play better than them, they shun the notion as mere speculation.

But God wants your life and mine to improve, to grow. The mere idea of stagnation in the Christian life should be, for the Christian, a foreign idea. Peter gives the illustration of babies growing up: "Like newborn infants, long for the pure spiritual milk, that by it you may grow up into salvation—if indeed you have tasted that the Lord is good" (1 Peter 2:2-3).
Again, this is evident in Philippians chapter one as Paul prays for the church:

> I thank my God in all my remembrance of you, always in every prayer of mine for you all making my prayer with joy, because of your

> partnership in the gospel from the first day until now. And I am sure of this, that he who began a good work in you will bring it to completion at the day of Jesus Christ. ~ Philippians 1:3-6

It doesn't matter what stage of development you're in or how far you've come in your Christian walk. The journey with Christ is always a transitional journey, moving you from one level of glory to the next, from a place of immaturity to that place of full maturity, from uncertainty to absolute confidence. Even the most seasoned and experienced veterans of the Christian life are still in a state of transitional growth. Or, as Proverbs 4:18 says, "But the path of the righteous is like the light of dawn, which shines brighter and brighter until full day."

Close… but not quite

On the fringe, you're not quite there. You haven't reached the green in actuality, though it seems as if you had. And in life, there are times when it seems that you're standing just on the fringe, you're not quite "in" but you can see the goal.

For many, being on the fringes of life has become such a comfortable condition that they never reach beyond themselves to actually strive for anything. Old goals and ancient dreams linger like faded memories and have been set aside for the more practical aspects of living. On the fringes of life, most Christians have turned away from the possibility that they can do more, be more and serve the Lord with greater success than they have before. Missionary dreams fade like the sunset before the final putt and become the story that never was. Ministry possibilities that once blossomed in the full light of hopeful anticipation drop their petals in sorrowful disappointments. All these things, and so many more, linger on the fringe.

There's a warning in the Old Testament concerning this state of being: ""Woe to those who are at ease in Zion, and to those who feel secure on the mountain of Samaria, the notable men of the first of the nations, to whom the house of Israel comes" (Amos 6:1). Are you at ease? Do you feel secure with minimal effort in your Christian life? Or, like the Apostle Paul, do you strive for greater heights, stepping off the fringes of your life to reach the goal? "Not that I have already obtained this or am already perfect, but I press on to make it my own, because Christ Jesus has made me his own" (Philippians 3:12).

No matter how you approach it, being on the fringe cannot be the place you choose to stop. It reminds me of a story of a competitive runner, going against others in a mile-long foot race. They ran upon a quarter-mile track: four laps and they're done. The runner, with great skill and swift strides quickly pulled away from the competition. Three laps in and he had already passed his competitors and determined to quit the race. Another runner finished the four laps and won the competition. When asked "Why did you stop?" the first runner said, "Well, I had beaten them three out of four laps and that should have been enough."

You don't get to the end until you complete the race. The hole is not finished till the putt goes in. What if you played in a four-round tournament and for the first three rounds you were in the lead. Do you stop? Of course not, you play through till the final putt or else there will be no possible victory.

Multiple Choice Options

What club do you select? A wedge… a putter… perhaps another club that you will use to get the ball rolling? This is the issue that many people have with being on the fringe. I remember watching a tournament when one of the players took his three-wood from the bag and, with great care and skill, barely tapped his ball and it rolled up to the hole. Such is life – filled with choices! People make choices every day about a whole host of things. Decisions, agendas and plans fill up our calendars and make life a frenetic and sometimes frantic desperation of choice. If I have my three kids in the car and ask what fast-food restaurant to eat lunch, I will invariably get three different answers! Choices… choices… choices!

The Christian life is no different. There are choices to be made, and they must be made for the purpose that God has designed. Every Sunday, however, millions of Christians choose convenience or conviction, and decide to forgo gathering with the church for worship. Many Christians choose greed over generosity and leave behind the call of God to participate in the regular offering. Hundreds will choose safety over sacrifice and never venture beyond the borders of their own comfort in order to reach out with the gospel and love of Christ. It's all about choice.

The classic and unmistakable words of Joshua, as he gives his final address to the people of Israel, declares with certainty the call to make the right choice. "And if it is evil in your eyes to serve the Lord, choose this day whom you will serve, whether the gods your fathers served in the region beyond the River, or the gods of the Amorites in whose land you dwell. But as for me and my house, we will serve the Lord" (Joshua 24:15).

But more than just in the religious realm of our lives, there are choices that must be made every day that will reflect the heart of a Christian. But for many, to make a choice often results in conflict.

Let me share an example from my life:

One summer, I promised to take my family to the annual Highland Games (A festival of Scottish heritage). It was an exciting time because I am a descendant of ancient highlanders, a clan of warriors whose motto is: "Disce Pati" or, "learn to suffer." My surname "Duncan" means "Dark Warrior." Perhaps that is why I preach the word of God with little concern for people's entertainment.

However, a ministry need rose up in the church. A longtime member of the community had died and though I was not delivering the message at the funeral, some members of the church wanted me to attend, and, you guessed it, the funeral was scheduled during the games. I now had a choice: do I take my family to the games or attend to the need of the church? Someone is destined for disappointment.

Welcome to the conflict.

To choose Christ is to choose a pathway that is set against the conflicting ideas and temptations of this world. Jesus faced the same choices that you and I must face – to follow in faithful obedience to the will of the Father in heaven or to determine to live for selfish agendas and purposes. In Matthew, chapter four, the iconic battle between Satan and the Son of God reached fevered pitch as the enemy of all that is good hit Jesus with every temptation. Finally, at the top of a mountain (so apropos for the climax of this great battle) Jesus lifted up His voice in absolute victory and said, "Be gone, Satan! For it is written, 'You shall worship the Lord your God and him only shall you serve'" (Matthew 4:10). Jesus set His feet upon the path of resolute determination to do nothing except that which was faithful to His Father.

So, the question is: what about you?

Are you just hanging about the fringes of life? Perhaps you've fallen short of the target. Maybe you were aiming for the green in one great sweeping shot and you missed it by that much (thank you, Maxwell Smart, Agent 86). And now, having missed the green, do you just determine to linger on the fringe? You have a choice to make, there's still a shot to take and you must decide to take it. Was there a purpose in your life given by God and it remains un-fulfilled? Did you try to make your way only to fall short? Now is not the time to give up or to remain complacent. Now is the time to size up your next shot, make a choice and get off the fringe

.

And… if you were wondering what choice I made in the earlier scenario… I took my family to the games.

Hole Six

The Hazards

OH, THEY'RE ALL around! Hazards are employed upon golf courses by their designers like land mines in a war. They come in all shapes and sizes, covering all manner of terrain and I'm sure bearing a grudge against any and every golfer who ever played the game. Sometimes they're obvious, as if they dare you to attempt the shot. Sometimes they're hidden away, a covert operative waiting like a camouflaged guerrilla warrior. But the fact remains, there are hazards all around and the best courses seem to boast the greatest ones.

One sunny afternoon (a rare find in my home state), I enjoyed a quiet round of golf with my son. The day was near the end and with long shadows cast upon the ground we stepped up to the 18th tee. A short par four waited, one I had birdied on numerous occasions. Just over three hundred yards and we were done. However, lurking between me and the green loomed a bunker - a sand trap - that might have been dug to specifications found somewhere in Dante's Inferno. It was so deep you could feel the heat from the Earth's molten core slowly melting your iron resolve.

My driver was my best club that day and I had hit the ball with rare precision. And now, 315 yards away, the flag flittered in the breeze, tempting me to try and drive the green. I hit the ball and that glorious sound of a well-struck shot echoed across the fairway. It soared high. Oh I would impress my son if I drive the green in one shot! I hear in my mind the delighted praise of an imagined gallery.

"Dad," my son said, snapping me back to reality and interrupting my internal revelry. "Hey dad, you're in the bunker." The bunker! It wasn't a bunker, it was a pit, a carved out cavernous hole that I'm sure once boasted a strip-mining operation.

But that's life. There are hazards strewn about the fairways we walk upon and those who strive after the highest, noblest aims will discover that the hazards are of the most severe difficulty. As you walk with Christ you will discover that the hazards increase along the way. Being a mature Christian does not minimize the risks, it just increases your capacity to handle them. There is a reason why the touring pros are successful on the most difficult courses: they have learned their lessons along the way. That is the gift of the hazards.

Those traps and pitfalls come through two agencies - self and others. Consider the words of the Psalms. Psalm 7:15, "He makes a pit, digging it out, and falls into the hole that he has made." Again, in Psalm 57:6, "They set a net for my steps; my soul was bowed down. They dug a pit in my way, but they have fallen into it themselves. Selah."

There are three things to consider as you look upon the hazards: some hazards you can recover from, some hazards you can't, and all hazards will take their toll.

Some Hazards You can Recover From

It was a choice. A simple decision lay before me as I peered out over the fairway to the green beyond. Hemmed in by a dense copse of trees on either side, the straight, narrow fairway harbored only one other difficulty. A bunker lay in wait on the right and in range for the amateur golfer. A simple lay-up shot and then a long iron to the green would have been the preferred choice, but I was striking the ball well that day.

Just to carry the hazard would take a shot of at least 285 yards. But if I could do it, all that remained was a simple up-and-down for a birdie! The wind gently whispered from the tee box with a promise to aid the ball's flight. Trees on either side of the fairway swayed in anticipation and a hushed moment fell upon the earth. I made my choice. With driver in hand, I planted my tee and took a mighty swing. The crack of the ball startled the birds and they scattered. My eyes followed the flight and it was glorious! Straight and true with a trajectory like a missile as it sailed into the shimmering sunlight.

I was certain to have cleared the bunker, but lost sight of my ball as it flew into the glare of the sun. I strode down the fairway alone, clubs in tow, to find my ball settled at the bottom of the bunker. It had hit the lip of the hazard and bounded back into the waiting sand. The ball was still in play, but now the going just became exceedingly difficult. I made a choice… and it was wrong.

I find that this is the reality of many of the hazards in life. Choices are made that lead to difficulty and cause many to struggle along the way. Your life is still "in play" but now the going has just become especially hard.

How many people have fallen victim to the notion of "trying?" Not trying to do great things with virtuous and valiant hearts, but trying - or rather, experimenting - with something that is surreptitiously sinful. We've all done it… we started with a small handful of potato chips thinking "this is all I'll take" and ended up devouring the bag without realizing it. All of us have fallen prey to the idea that we, unlike everyone else, can avoid that trap! One drink does not an alcoholic make; one glance does not plummet a heart into the depravity of pornography; one puff will not create a drug addict. Yep… we've all done something stupid because we thought we were above the reach of its enticement.

The Lord Jesus gives this clear warning from Matthew 26:41, "Watch and pray that you may not enter into temptation. The spirit indeed is willing, but the flesh is weak."

Again, God's word warns us, "For by the grace given to me I say to everyone among you not to think of himself more highly than he ought to think, but to think with sober judgment, each according to the measure of faith that God has assigned" (Romans 12:3).

In your life, there will be moments of choice set before you - a choice to either entertain sin or turn aside from it. The thought that you or I can simply "dabble" in the shallows of some sinful experience without suffering the consequences of those choices will invariably lead to the trap that's waiting.

Perhaps you are, even now, caught up in the trap of sin. Yes, it will take some effort to escape. But, as God's word says in 1 John 1:9, "If we confess our sins, he is faithful and just to forgive us our sins and to cleanse us from all unrighteousness."

Some Hazards You can't Recover From

There is nothing more doleful than the sound of a golf ball splashing into the water hazard. It's gone… it's lost… it is forever beyond your reach and the only thing left to do is take the penalty and try again.

I took my son out golfing. It was working to be a bright, clear day as the fog that had settled on the course began to burn off in the light of the morning. Stray drifts of mist sauntered across the fairway, seemingly relaxed in their tranquil passage across the greens. Now my son was just a beginner, a neophyte - just a novice - at this game. Yet, on this particularly peaceful day, he was striking the ball with much-improved accuracy. Until that fateful hole…

A water hazard stood between him and the green. It was designed to protect the left side of the green and, where I had approached the green from the right, my son was, invariably, on the left. And, to add a bit of a twist to his fate, he's a lefty with a tendency to slice.

But he had been hitting the ball fairly straight, and his distance was decent. So, with much courage and an improved opinion of his game, he took his shot - right for the pin. Unfortunately, you guessed it, the ball splashed down like Apollo 13. No amount of his desperate pleading while the ball was in the air could have nudged it beyond the water. He had to take a drop. A lost shot. With a sigh of resignation to the circumstances, he dropped his ball near the water, took a shot and scuttled it right into to pond! Another lost shot. Exasperation filled his features and he nearly threw his club in the water after the ball.

After a deep breath, he hit his next shot and finally made the green. On a par four, he shot a nine.

My son learned the lesson that all of us have learned on the course. A great round can be flustered by a bad hole - even by a bad shot. One bad shot often takes two to recover, and so it is in life.

All of us make mistakes, but some are far more hazardous than others. Like we learned above, some hazards you can recover from. Then there are those where you simply must take your punishment and move on. God's mercy is great and will cover over our sins with His forgiveness in Christ. But God did not necessarily come to save us from the circumstances. He does not treat us as our sins deserve (Psalm 103:10), but there will be consequences for choices that may not be easily remedied. You may have to, as the adage says, "take your medicine and move on."

One of these tragic hazards is found in the epic story of David and Bathsheba. You can read the entirety of David's failing in 2 Samuel, chapter eleven. But, the consequences of the choice that he made held ramifications for the rest of his kingship. In chapter twelve of that same book, the prophet Nathan rebukes King David, confronting him with his failure and telling him of the consequences:

> Why have you despised the word of the Lord, to do what is evil in his sight? You have struck down Uriah the Hittite with the sword and have taken his wife to be your wife and have killed him with the sword of the Ammonites. Now therefore the sword shall never depart from your

> house, because you have despised me and have taken the wife of Uriah the Hittite to be your wife.' Thus says the Lord, 'Behold, I will raise up evil against you out of your own house. And I will take your wives before your eyes and give them to your neighbor, and he shall lie with your wives in the sight of this sun. For you did it secretly, but I will do this thing before all Israel and before the sun.'" ~ 2 Samuel 12:9-12

What an absolute miss-hit! And, as per the prophet's rebuke, all these things did happen to King David. With humble repentance, David confessed his sin against God. In His mercy, God "put away" (forgave) David's sin and spared the king's life (see verse 13). But that did not alleviate the consequences. David "took his medicine" and then he played on.

All Hazards Take their Toll

Years ago I was told a fantastical lie. I was told that golf, like life, is a game of "do-overs." That's not true. There is no do-over in life. For all of my wishing to go back in time and try to make a better go of it, I cannot change anything that happened in my past. The only thing I can do is to take the moment I'm in right now and make the best shot available to me.

Perhaps you've landed in a bunker in your life. You may have done something stupid, caused grief or pain, committed a sin, or made a choice that put you in a position that is difficult. You still have a shot, but it will be a bit more difficult. You'll have to own up to it and go forward from there.

Or, maybe, you have fallen so far that you fear you're lost and without a shot left to you. You have entered a hazard that demands payment. There's no escaping the hazard, there's no getting out. All that's left for you to do is to "take your medicine" and, with humble repentance, prepare to play your next shot. I've known men who, because of a foolish choice or sinful life, found themselves in jail, prison, homeless, penniless, with failed marriages, bankrupt businesses and so on. They are in a hazard and there's no denying the truth of it. Own up to the sin, repent and learn from your mistake. Then, in humility, get ready to try again.

I want you to read Luke 23:39-43.

> One of the criminals who were hanged railed at him, saying, "Are you not the Christ? Save yourself and us!" But the other rebuked him, saying, "Do you not fear God, since you are under the same sentence of condemnation? And we indeed justly, for we are receiving the due reward of our deeds; but this man has done nothing wrong." And he said, "Jesus, remember me when you come into your kingdom." And he said to him, "Truly, I say to you, today you will be with me in Paradise."

Think about it like this: the second thief on the cross, who had made such a mess of his life that he was sentenced to death, had a final moment to make one more glorious shot and it turned out to be a spiritual hole-in-one!

Hole Seven

Out of Bounds

I FIND IT odd how many golf courses I've played on that have an out-of-bounds bordering a cow pasture. I guess that comes from playing in more rural settings, but there is nothing quite like hitting a shanked shot and watching it come to rest inches away from some bovine's hoof.

But, having grown up for a brief time on a farm, I'm not all that distressed with large farm animals casually grazing just a few feet away from me. So why, then, is it out of bounds? I guess it's designed to protect the surrounding area, mark the edges of the course and provide a greater level of difficulty for those of us who tend to approach the fairway with a heightened level of avoidance.

My current home course has a greater measure of boundaries because it is nestled within a pristine community of the upper-middleclass. There are houses lining the fairways and all their backyards are marked as out-of-bounds. It makes sense to me because it helps protect the manicured lawns. I mean, who would want a hack golfer coming onto their property and whack a six iron into their sod, leaving a divot the size of a moon crater? Okay… I would, but that's beside the point. And, anyway, there are moon-crater divots dotting my backyard already.

But, more to the point, there is a boundary, an out-of-bounds barrier between the acreage of playable land and the vast swath of unexplored terrain beyond the stakes, that no-man's-land called… well… the rest of the earth. It sits outside the golf course and is often the place from where no golf ball has ever returned.

Much like the white-staked markers of a golf course, in life God has some "out-of-bounds" stakes that mark the limit of His permission. God is the creator of all things – the architect and course designer of life and the universe. He created the boundaries of the atom; He designed the limits of the sky; He set the heavens in their places and put restrictions on all of life.

I'd like you to consider what it says in the book of Job:

> Then the Lord answered Job out of the whirlwind and said: "Who is this that darkens counsel by words without knowledge? Dress for action like a man; I will question you, and you make it known to me. "Where were you when I laid the foundation of the earth? Tell me, if you have understanding. Who determined its measurements—surely you know! Or who stretched the line upon it? On what were its bases sunk, or who laid its cornerstone, when the morning stars sang together and all the sons of God shouted for joy? "Or who shut in the sea with doors when it burst out from the womb, when I made clouds its garment and thick darkness its swaddling band, and prescribed limits for it and set bars and doors, and said, 'Thus far shall you come, and no farther, and here shall your proud waves be stayed'?" ~ Job 38:1-11

The simple truth is: God is the one who laid the foundations of the earth; He is the one who established the very elements of life. It was He who created not only all that we enjoy—He created you and me too! So it stands to reason that He is the one who also has the right and the authority to establish the boundaries of life.

The First "Out-of-Bounds" Marker

I remember the first time I went to play golf with my dad. I was a teenager, full of myself and empty of skills. My dad, well, he could play golf! He often shot in the low seventies and the upper sixties in a round, and he wanted to instill his love of the game in me.

So off we went, meeting up with some of his playing friends as we stepped onto the first tee. He tried to give me instructions on how to swing the club, how to grip it, and where to aim. I was, admittedly, rather reluctant to receive any instructions from him. I should just be able to step up, whack the ball and move on to the next shot - it ought to have been a birdie festival!

My first shot was horrendous! Way to the right. It was called a slice, but was rather more shaped like a crooked banana, sailing over a low fence and down a paved road. Bounce… bounce… bounce… and it was long gone. I'm certain it's still rolling somewhere on the highway. Yes, even for me, it was obvious I could never retrieve that ball. So I teed up another and with a mighty swing, I sliced again! This time, however, it missed the road and the low fence line and nestled in some thick grass.

We walked up to my ball's location and I retrieved a club to smack the unruly thing from its hiding place.

"Wait a minute!" called my dad. "You can't hit that ball."

I was stunned. It was right in front of me and I was certain that I could, indeed, hit the silly thing. I shook my head and ignored my dad.

"Son!" he cried out again. "You can't hit that ball… you're out of bounds."

I looked up and to my wild surprise I stood on the wrong side of a set of markers depicting the edge of the course. Yep, I was out of bounds. But what did it matter? The ball was in front of me, I could simply ignore a minor rule like being out of bounds, couldn't I? But my dad was a stickler for the rules and he marched me back to the first tee, had me re-tee my ball, and take another shot. He taught me that day no matter how easy it might be to break them, there is no escaping the rules.

At the very beginning of humanity, God established a simple distinction between what was "in play" and what was "out-of-bounds." In another chapter we will look at the rules more closely, but in the Garden of Eden God established the parameters for life.

> The Lord God took the man and put him in the Garden of Eden to work it and keep it. And the Lord God commanded the man, saying, "You may surely eat of every tree of the garden, but of the tree of the knowledge of good and evil you shall not eat, for in the day that you eat of it you shall surely die." ~ Genesis 2:15-17

It was simple, Adam and Eve had the run of the garden. They were called upon by God to work and keep it and they could enjoy all the bounty it provided. But there was one place out of bounds – the tree in the center of the garden called the "tree of the knowledge of good and evil."

Boy did they ever slice it out of bounds! In one chapter (though we don't know how much time passed between chapter's two and three of Genesis) Adam and Eve listened to the serpent that had slithered into the garden and convinced them they could play outside the boundary that God had established. Because of their sin, all of humanity was thrust into a condition where we are all "out of bounds." Every one of us have fallen short of the glory of God and are in a state of sin (Romans 3:23).

A Chance to Recover Your Life

What happened on that day in the Garden of Eden caused a catastrophic failure for all mankind. When you're out-of-bounds, you can't simply "play it as it lies." The opportunity for that shot is lost and it must be recovered in only one way – go back and take another shot.

But how do we do that? In golf it's easy: pick up your ball if you can find it and re-hit the shot, or use a provisional shot if you cannot. As you read in the previous chapter, life is not as simple as just living a "do-over." And when you're out of bounds, it is far less so. How do you recover from sin? How do you pick up the pieces of a broken and fallen life when it seems that there is no recovery? There is only one way – the mercy and grace of Jesus Christ.

On that fateful first day of my golfing experience, I hit it out of bounds. I also was able to begin again. Not a do-over, but a renewal – a recovery of a failed moment to try once more. And in Christ Jesus you have the opportunity to start again. Romans 6:23 reads, "For the wages of sin is death, but the free gift of God is eternal life in Christ Jesus our Lord." Again, in Romans 8:32, "He who did not spare his own Son but gave him up for us all, how will he not also with him graciously give us all things?"

Consider the words of 1 John:

> In this the love of God was made manifest among us, that God sent his only Son into the world, so that we might live through him. In this is love, not that we have loved God but that he loved us and sent his Son to be the propitiation for our sins. ~ 1 John 4:9-10

If you are reading this and you are not a Christian, I will plainly tell you - you are out of bounds. Without the mercy of God in Christ Jesus and His forgiveness of your sins, you do not have any hope of eternal life.

John 3:16 is, perhaps, the most quoted text from the Bible: "For God so loved the world, that he gave his only Son, that whoever believes in him should not perish but have eternal life." Two verses later, however, gives the clear indication of how far out-of-bounds everyone is: "Whoever believes in him is not condemned, but whoever does not believe in him is condemned already, because he has not believes in the name of the only Son of God" (John 3:18, italics added).

God does not want anyone to remain outside of His grace and mercy. He does not want you to stay "out-of-bounds." But you have to come back into the field of play, back onto the course of life the only way made available, and that is through Jesus Christ. Repent and receive the Lord Jesus. Yield yourself to Him in humble gratitude for what He did to give you hope and a chance at life again.

Paul said it quite clearly:

> "Therefore, O King Agrippa, I was not disobedient to the heavenly vision, but declared first to those in Damascus, then in Jerusalem and throughout all the region of Judea, and also to the Gentiles, that they should repent and turn to God, performing deeds in keeping with their repentance." ~ Acts 26:19-20

Three very simple things: repent, return to God and show it by the life you live going forward. If you are out-of-bounds in your life, this is the way to get back on the field of play. We'll see these three things again in a later chapter.

The Markers haven't Moved

I want to close out this chapter with a simple truth: the out-of-bounds lines have never moved.

There are those who believe that the Old Testament has a different set of boundaries than the New Testament of the Bible. That's not the case. Both the Old and New Testaments point out this simple fact: all of mankind has sinned and fallen short of God's perfect design. Both the Old and New Testaments proclaim that the only way to return is through repentance and faith.

As observed in the text from Acts 26, so you will see the same thought in Isaiah 30:15, "In returning [repentance] and rest you shall be saved; in quietness and in trust [obedient faith] shall be your strength." The same understanding of repentance and faith mentioned in the Old Testament is made even clearer in the New Testament.

A better way of comprehending this is to view the Old and New Testaments of the Bible as a complete anthology of the work of God for the salvation of man, culminating in the death, burial and resurrection of Jesus and finalized in His return. There is not a different standard, nor are there different boundaries. God is the architect and the One who established what is "out-of-bounds."

And if, right now, you are outside of faith in Jesus Christ… you are "out of bounds."

Hole Eight

The Clubs

EVERY OCCUPATION HAS their "tools of the trade." Golf is no exception.

Trying to describe a golf club to a non-player can be a problematic experience for the golfer. And, over the years, the club has so transformed in appearance and effect that if you were to take a club from even 40 years ago and compare it to the modern rendition of equipment, it would be a remarkable difference.

I've often wondered what would happen if I could take a modern-day professional golfer and transport them back in time to play against the greats of the past, all-the-while using period equipment. Or, better yet, I wonder how far a man like Bobby Jones would go if he stepped up to the tee box today, with all the improvements made in modern equipment.

The evolution of the golf club has certainly aided my game! I remember when I played with my dad, how I would pull out one of my "woods" and it was still actually made of wood! It was a steel shaft with a persimmon head. I know… hard to believe. I actually own a hickory stick golf club—not a replica—though I've never actually used it. But, to tell you the truth, I have been tempted. Yet, to look at the hickory club and match it against a forged carbon steel club of today, there is no comparison.

The growth of the game of golf, and the improvements in equipment along the way, has spurred multitudes to embrace the delights of striking a clean drive off the tee. I am glad that golf is a sport that can allow for the growth of technology and yet still maintain a strong adherence to the spirit of the game. So, while things continue to change - they still stay the same.

The church is no exception to the advancement of "technology." During the days of the early church, the gathering of God's people found themselves in homes, sometimes in caves, to hear the proclamation of God's word.
Today most Christians enjoy the comfort of clean buildings and climate control, while the bands of this era minister the music

of the day. The Bible has not changed in all these years, but there are so many aids and helps now to study God's word that it is only by choice a Christian fails to grow in their knowledge of it. In the centuries past, Christians were hard pressed to find anyone with a copy of the Word of God, let alone have at their fingertips the concordances, commentaries, study guides and notes from theologians of countless generations available at the press of a button. Right now, I have at my disposal thirty-two Bible translations that can render for me a wealth of understanding—and all on the computer I am currently using to write this paragraph!

But… as things change with the times, so the truth MUST remain the same. No amount of growth in the game of golf concerning technological advancements has dented the simple and time-tested method and measure of play. You still need to "play the ball where it lies" and "play the course as you find it." And no amount of change to the technological tools of the church will ever change the basic reality that Christianity is still all about Christ.

It's a limited set.
You've got fourteen clubs to choose from. Oh, If only that were the case when some hackers are on the course.

On a glorious Spring day I departed in the morning for the closest course available. I had a few hours available to me and I wanted to get a round of golf in before my next scheduled appointment. It's true that I rarely take a day off. More like, I take a few hours off on a day during the week and use that

time to take a walk around the grand greenway of a golf course. And that was my day on this particular day.
Anyway, I strolled up to the first tee and found another lone golfer waiting to propel his ball down the long stretch before us. We joined up and toured the course together. However, he was a man of great indecision and it showed in the selection of clubs in his bag.

Yes, there are fourteen clubs allowed (according to the rules) and this man must have had at least twenty in his bag. Every iron available, including a one-iron, four wedges, three woods two drivers and two putters littered his bag and weighed down his walk along the course. So, as we journeyed, we came upon his ball and he stood staring with wondering eyes at the green far off in the distance. He rummaged through his selection of clubs, pulled one out, put it back with a shake of his head and took out another one. This went on for several minutes and I came to understand at least one reason why the fourteen club rule is in place!

In your walk with Christ, there are many "tools" of the trade that you can put into your bag. But I believe that the Bible gives us at least four that are definite requirements for a faithful walk and successful life with Christ. We harken back to the early church and look to discover the four elements of devotion that the first new believers devoted themselves to, with a quick observation on how to implement each devotion into your routine.

Four Devotions - Acts 2:42

"And they devoted themselves to the apostles' teaching and the fellowship, to the breaking of bread and the prayers."

➢ Apostles Teaching - Devoted to the Word of God

This is where it begins—this is your "driver." Without a true devotion to the Word of God, there will be no real foundation that can be trusted. But this foundation cannot only be knowledge of the Word of God, that's just where it starts. The true foundation is built through obedience to the Word of God.

This is how discipleship is built: "Everyone then who hears these words of mine and does them will be like a wise man who built his house on the rock" (Matthew 7:24).

The Great Commission of God concludes with this: "…teaching them to observe [obey] all that I have commanded you" (Matthew 28:20).

Love is seen in obedience: "If anyone loves me, he will keep [obey] my word, and my Father will love him, and we will come to him and make our home with him." (John 14:23).

✓ *Commit to participating in a regular Bible study*

➢ Fellowship - Devoted to the People of God

In fellowship you discover your "woods and irons." God has called us to live in fellowship. There are Christians today that harbor the idea that they can be the "Lone Ranger" Christian and live their faith without the structure and support of the church. But God has purposed that only together will each individual Christian grow and develop as God intended.

Through fellowship we grow and become mature: "…from whom the whole body, joined and held together by every joint with which it is equipped, when each part is working properly, makes the body grow so that it builds itself up in love" (Ephesians 4:16).

It provides the means of mutual encouragement: "…not neglecting to meet together, as is the habit of some, but encouraging one another, and all the more as you see the Day drawing near" (Hebrews 10:25).

Though gathering with the church does not save you, it is evidence of real faith: "They went out from us, but they were not of us; for if they had been of us, they would have continued with us. But they went out, that it might become plain that they all are not of us" (1 John 2:19).

- ✓ *Commit to gathering with the church every Sunday unless God prevents it*

- ➢ Breaking of Bread – Devoted to the Worship of God

Here you find your "wedges," that which brings you closer to God. The issue of breaking bread together is two-fold. First, it is the remembrance that Christ has given us when He said, "Do this in remembrance of me" (Luke 22:19). It is an expression of worship and a reminder of why we have salvation – the sacrifice of Christ. Second, it is an expression of sacrifice toward those around us by bringing them into our homes to "break bread" with us, especially those who cannot repay.

It is a call to self-examination: "Let a person examine himself, then, and so eat of the bread and drink of the cup." (1 Corinthians 11:28).

It reflects the generous heart of God: "But when you give a feast, invite the poor, the crippled, the lame, the blind, and you will be blessed, because they cannot repay you. For you will be repaid at the resurrection of the just" (Luke 14:13-14).

Christ is honored in this: "And the King will answer them, 'Truly, I say to you, as you did it to one of the least of these my brothers, you did it to me'" (Matthew 25:40).

- ✓ *Commit to worshiping God through personal sacrifice toward someone who cannot repay*

- ➢ Prayer – Devoted to a Life with God

Here is the "putter," where you get closest to God. In all healthy relationships communication is critical. No marriage truly grows in depth and happiness without it. No family can survive when communication is lost. And no believer in Christ will have any hope of truly knowing and living in a relationship with the Lord if prayer is not an essential devotion in their lives.

Prayer is personal communion with God: "But when you pray, go into your room and shut the door and pray to your Father who is in secret. And your Father who sees in secret will reward you" (Matthew 6:6).

Prayer should fill the fellowship of God's people: "So Peter was kept in prison, but earnest prayer for him was made to God by the church" (Acts 12:5).

Prayer is essential for spiritual readiness: "...praying at all times in the Spirit, with all prayer and supplication. To that end keep alert with all perseverance, making supplication for all the saints" (Ephesians 6:18).

- ✓ *Commit to daily prayer at home and at least once a month with your church*

It is essential to have the right clubs available and to know how to use them. I love it when I pull out a club from my bag and know, without question, that I will be able to hit the ball with confidence. That comes through practice and only through practice and always through practice. So it is with your Christian life. You need to know your Christian tools. Implement these four devotions into your routine of faith and practice until they become habit, eventually becoming who you are as a Christian.

Which one… which one?

I have a club in my bag that I carry around for sentimental reasons. It is called a "lil' david."It has the loft of a putter, the shaft length of a three-wood and the angle of an iron and I cannot, for the life of me, figure out what it's used for. But it belonged to my late father who carried it with him as he played and now it belongs to me. I've tried to use it to punch out from under trees or to get the ball rolling from the fringe. I even took a mighty swing with it from the tee box only to have my hands numbed from the pain-wracking vibrations of the club! So, there it sits in my bag. Unused. Sentimental. And I doubt that I will ever part with it.

But everyone carries around frivolous items in their golf bag. Old scorecards, a collection of pencils, broken tees and various other paraphernalia litter the pockets and recesses of a person's bag. The problem surfaces when they get weighed down with such items. Those items clutter everything up and make it hard to find what you need. I knew of a man who tried to pull out a golf club and it was stuck! Okay, that man was me. The reason my club stuck fast in the bag was due to a broken club head at the bottom that wedged in-between two clubs and jammed them together. At that moment I knew it was time to clear out the clutter.

There are some things that get hauled around in life that people should truly reconsider keeping. They are sentimental things, unused things, or simply things that have no place in the arsenal of the Christian golf bag. Old habits that are not necessarily sinful, and old sins that don't seem very harmful, clutter up and clatter around in life and take up precious space that weighs the life down.

But the Bible says in Hebrews 12:1, "Therefore, since we are surrounded by so great a cloud of witnesses, let us also lay aside every weight, and sin which clings so closely, and let us run with endurance the race that is set before us."

Just like my "lil' david" took up space or the broken piece of a club got things stuck, so there is spiritual clutter in life and, as the verse above says, we must "lay aside" everything that hinders and dispose of all known sin through confession and repentance in order to run with endurance.

But you might be thinking to yourself that those "extra" things in your life are useful. As the man with twenty clubs in his bag, he considered every one of them an absolute necessity for his game. I want you to consider these words from the Apostle Paul:

> If with Christ you died to the elemental spirits of the world, why, as if you were still alive in the world, do you submit to regulations—"Do not handle, Do not taste, Do not touch" (referring to things that all perish as they are used)—according to human precepts and teachings? These have indeed an appearance of wisdom in promoting self-made religion and asceticism and severity to the body, but they are of no value in

> stopping the indulgence of the flesh. ~ Colossians 2:20-23

The tendency is to add such self-made religious expressions in order to try and get a handle on the sinful condition of the heart. In the end, however, you end up trusting more in your religious codes and creeds and eventually abandon the faith-fellowship with Jesus Christ. Jesus becomes the figurehead, so to speak, of your new-found religion. And, thus, so many religious orders are born that do not worship Christ but a rather worship their own creed.

One of the things that I truly believe is that the Bible is the sole authority for our faith. Keep it simple, as the old adage says, and do not clutter up your bag with an assortment of things that do not have any room or any reason in the Christian life. The tools you need are already given you by Christ and are found in His word. Take them and learn to use them to their full advantage. Or, as Paul says to the Philippians, "Only let us hold true to what we have attained" (Philippians 3:16).

Hole Nine

The Ball

IT WAS A cold, wet day. The night had seen a squall come through and the course was doused with a drenching rain. Dawn broke, and with the morning I rose and steeled myself to face the chill, damp conditions.

Heavy clouds rolled across the sky, with a trickle of moisture falling through the atmosphere and dancing upon the ground. Most of the rain had ended and only a dismal, misanthropic drizzle continued as I arrived on the course. The parking lot was vacant. It felt like that scene in the movie "Vacation" as they pulled into the parking lot and noticed every spot was available. Not one person had decided to golf that day—literally, I was the only one. I half expected to see a "closed" sign on the door.

But I entered the clubhouse and was greeted with a display of surprised looks from the three people working that day. Sideways glances and quizzical stares crossed their faces as I approached. Finally, as I stood before the counter to pay for my round of golf, the clerk asked me, "What are you doing here on a day like this?"

I was there to play golf! I didn't mind a little drizzle and most golfers in Washington State know that if you want to play during the year, you're going to have to get used to playing in the rain. But it was cold that day, and the damp, chilly conditions made it increasingly unpleasant. So, I smiled and then asked to see the basket of "used" golf balls for sale. I needed a few - for I was bound to lose several along the way.

At that time in my experience, I was a "Pinnacle" man. Now, this is no endorsement for any golf ball company, and I still use them on occasion, though I have switched to Callaway balls now. Anyway, I rummaged through the basket and picked out about six that I thought would serve me well along the way. The clerk gave me a bewildered look as I spent time tracking through the basket and asked me, "What does it matter on a day like today which ball you use?
"

What? I looked up and spoke, with no uncertainty in my voice. "Golf," I said, "is all about the ball."

And, in truth, it really is. Not the type of ball you use—for there are many. High spin, low spin, hex dimples, round dimples, solid core, liquid core - who knows, maybe even iron core! Nike, Callaway, Titleist, Pinnacle, Srixon, Bridgestone and the list goes on and on and on…

But golf is all about the ball. Everything you do is to make the ball go farther, land softer, roll truer. You practice fading the ball and drawing the ball. You dread slicing the ball or hooking the ball. And you count every time you hit the ball. Everything you try, every coach you hear, every round you play is simply and ultimately about hitting that ball. And according to some interesting probability statistics, there are over 2000 golf balls in the air every second![1]
In many endeavors in life there is that singular truth, that one all-encompassing reality that establishes the parameters for all other purposes. KFC was all about chicken, Baskin Robins was all about ice cream, Microsoft was all about the computer and the list goes on. In fact, those who succeed often discover that one golden thread of singular purpose that runs through everything and unites a variety of efforts into one, cohesive pursuit.

And, in this, Christianity is no exception. Many view the Christian faith in a variety of shades. Some see it as a kind religion that takes care of people. Others view it as merely a

---

[1] https://www.quora.com/How-many-golf-balls-are-in-the-air-right-now-world-wide

Sunday event, a gathering of people performing a ritualistic religion. Some even view Christianity as a political movement. Despite all that, there is a golden thread that all things must be tied to, a singular truth that unites everything called "Christian." Without this one truth, Christianity is pointless – like KFC without the chicken or like playing golf without the ball.

It's all about Christ.

This seems a simple truth, but when you let it sink in for a moment you begin to realize how absolutely vital this statement is. Christianity without Christ is religion without reason, faith without foundation, and hope without anything to hold. If you call yourself a Christian and do not know Jesus Christ as Savior and Lord, you do not recognize Him for who He is and trust Him for what He has done, you are fooling yourself.

But who is Jesus? The Bible gives ample evidence to the person of Jesus. All you have to do is pick up a Bible and read it. But, you must not rely on your imagination of Jesus or the world's definition of Jesus. You must go to the source – the revealed word of God. In Matthew 16:13 Jesus asked that very question: "Who do people say that the Son of Man is?" Ultimately the Lord brought the question directly to the disciples and asked, "But who do you say that I am?" And the Lord brings that question to your attention as well, and it is the most important question ever asked: who is Jesus? For if He is as the Bible reveals, then all of life must be brought under His authority and lived in obedience to His word.

Consider what the Lord Jesus said:

> "And the Father who sent me has himself borne witness about me. His voice you have never heard, his form you have never seen, and you do not have his word abiding in you, for you do not believe the one whom he has sent. You search the Scriptures because you think that in them you have eternal life; and it is they that bear witness about me, yet you refuse to come to me that you may have life." ~ John 5:37-40

Simply studying the Bible without finding Jesus is to deny the very purpose of God's word and to abandon the means of true salvation.

When asked, "show us the Father," Jesus declared that if anyone had seen Him, they had seen the Father (John 14:8-9). Prior to that, in His own self-description, Jesus explains He is the "Way, the Truth and the Life" (John 14:6). And from that description let's discover why.

- **The Way: Because We are Lost**

So often we want faith to be coupled together with some kind of "seven-step program" that gives us everything we need to make our way to heaven and will keep us in control as we strive to get there. But Jesus did not come to simply show us the way, He is the way. Like a search-and-rescue captain, Jesus comes to you to lead you out of sin and into righteousness, out of death and into life. And He does this because, without question: We are lost!

Those three words, filled with fear and dread, bring a sense of desperation. If you have ever been lost, you understand the terror that can accompany such a situation. You need someone to come and find you, to rescue you and lead you out. Help signs are left on beaches, smoke signals are wafted in the air, all to get the attention of someone, anyone, who can come and find you. Yet people who do not believe they are lost will fail to cry out to God to be found. Only when you know you're lost will you seek the means of rescue.

Jesus is the way, and this understanding is echoed by the prophet: Isaiah 35:8, "And a highway shall be there, and it shall be called the Way of Holiness; the unclean shall not pass over it. It shall belong to those who walk on the way; even if they are fools, they shall not go astray."

- **The Truth: Because We Believed Lies**

All of us have either been that friend on the course trying to offer advice or been subjected to the advice of those who play along with us. The problem I've always found is: everyone has a different understanding of what is needed. I won't deny that my game needs expert advice! And though my friends who play the game can give some great suggestions, the opinion of casual players will never elevate my skills.

It is the same with Christianity. Jesus is the truth, yet all around us are the voices of opinion telling us a variety of faulty information and failed wisdom. The knowledge of the truth has been revealed in Christ yet people refuse to follow Him. Why? Because most people would rather believe a comfortable lie than submit to the convicting truth of God. Jesus came as the revelator of truth – the embodiment of all that is God so that we could know the truth and be set free from the futility of lies. John 8:31-32 brings this to light: "So Jesus said to the Jews who had believed him, 'If you abide in my word, you are truly my disciples, and you will know the truth, and the truth will set you free.'"

Again we find God speaking in Isaiah 45:19, "I did not speak in secret, in a land of darkness; I did not say to the offspring of Jacob, 'Seek me in vain.' I the Lord speak the truth; I declare what is right."

- **The Life: Because We are Dead**

I've played alongside some good golfers—scratch golfers who could make the ball nearly dance in the air and fly with such precision as to leave me in a state of futile despair. Now, I've hit a few shots in my life. I've chipped in for an eagle, hit a huge drive straight off the tee (340 yards), putted a-more-than fifty-footer for birdie and hit a par five in two with a tap-in eagle remaining. And, sitting here as I recall all of those shots, most, I must admit, were accidental. At least they were not the norm. And I am certain that I cannot compare my game to the greats who have played before or are playing now. So, if sin means "missing the mark" then, I must confess, as a golfer - I am a sinner.

I will tell you this quite clearly - you and I have no idea how far we've strayed from that state of purity and innocence that Adam and Eve experienced in the Garden of Eden before the fall. This life we live, however meaningful and magnificent in this world, is a shadow and a far cry from the life that could have been without sin. The sinful state is death. Everyone has been born in such a state - decaying our way to eternity. Death does not exist in the company of God, so the only way to enter into God's presence is to have life - and that life is found in Christ Jesus. He gives it freely to all who will humbly ask. If the sinful state is death, the redeemed state is life!

The one hope we have is the redemption of God in Christ. As it says in Isaiah 53:11, "Out of the anguish of his soul he shall see and be satisfied; by his knowledge shall the righteous one, my servant, make many to be accounted righteous, and he shall bear their iniquities."

It's all about Jesus. He is the singular distinction between all the religions of the world and Christianity. Every church, whether liturgical, ecumenical, evangelical, protestant, etc. must have as their reason for existence the Son of God, the Savior of the world: the Lord Jesus Christ. If you are in a church or have a Christian faith where Jesus is merely a figurehead and not the exalted Head, now is the time to change your thinking about Jesus, and acknowledge that He is the King of kings and Lord of lords, the Almighty. Let the following words of 1 John sink into your heart as you come to grips with this truth.

1 John 5:20, "And we know that the Son of God has come and has given us understanding, so that we may know him who is true; and we are in him who is true, in his Son Jesus Christ. He is the true God and eternal life."

Hole Ten

Missed Shots

I HAD TO re-tee the ball.

You've been there. I've been there. Everyone, even the pros have been there. With the first swing, the crazed, dimpled projectile veered off course and vanished into the nether-sphere of trees and brush. It was lost, long lost. So, after a sigh of resignation and a moment to regain my composure, I steeled my will to make the next one count. I swung with such determination that the ball flew off the head of the golf club like a missile. It was that perfect sound. You know the sound I'm talking about—that perfect sound when the ball hits squarely on the clubface (amazing thing to do for a round ball to hit something "squarely") and soars into the air with unparalleled accuracy. Down the fairway it went bounding along till it rested just off to the left. My next shot was a sweeping draw around a tree, landing on the green! Two putts later and I got… a bogey. Sigh.

All the great shots that came after that miss-hit were nice, but I would have preferred a par or a birdie. And, just because the remaining shots were spectacular, I could not simply dismiss the first one. No do-overs. Just keep playing on.

I've heard golf described as a game of misses, and the best players in the world simply know how to miss better than the rest. I think it's true. There is no one who actually plays the perfect round of golf. Yes, some will endure endless rounds of frightfully horrific shots and others will soar through the rarefied air of one quality shot after another. But a perfect round of golf would consist of every par three as a hole in one, every par four in two, etc. There would be little fear of the bunkers or groves of trees planted in the middle of fairways. Facing water hazards or the dreaded out-of-bounds markers would bring no trepidation. But no one—and it does not matters how good they are—has ever played the perfect round of golf.

I had one Christian tell me, "You know, pastor… perfection is not all that it's cracked up to be." Wow! I had never met a perfect person. But there, standing before me, was a man who considered himself on the upper end of the measuring stick of

God. Granted, he needed to overlook his lack of humility, his indifference to others, his unrestrained effort to show everyone how good he actually was, his low consideration of all who were around him, and many other attributes that were less than a hole-in-one kind of life. But overlook all that and sure... he was perfect! His problem (which he confessed): he was bored with trying to maintain his perfection. He watched the world swirling around him and decided they were having all the fun, enjoying all the "rides" and playing with all the sins available to them. While in his self-imposed asceticism, he endured grueling day after grueling day of monotony.

But not even he was perfect, despite his own opinion of himself.

All Have Sinned

This simple statement is a truth that everyone must understand. God has established a standard of righteousness for humanity. It is not an external but an internal condition that the Almighty seeks, for God knows that when the heart is right, the entire life will follow suit. Even as Jesus stated while chastising the Pharisees:

> "Woe to you, scribes and Pharisees, hypocrites! For you clean the outside of the cup and the plate, but inside they are full of greed and self-indulgence. You blind Pharisee! First clean the inside of the cup and the plate, that the outside also may be clean." ~ Matthew 23:25-26

Consider the message of God to the prophet Samuel when the search for a new king was underway.

> But the Lord said to Samuel, "Do not look on his appearance or on the height of his stature, because I have rejected him. For the Lord sees not as man sees: man looks on the outward appearance, but the Lord looks on the heart." ~ 1 Samuel 16:7

I believe everyone knows they have an internal situation that is wrong. Every man and woman on this spinning planet has entertained bad thoughts, evil intents, anger toward their fellow man, even hatred. Lust and envy clutter the heart and pride covers it like a blanket. The Scriptures clearly teach that there are none righteous –no, not one (Romans 3:10) and that all have sinned and fallen short of God's glory (Romans 3:23). Take a glance at how even our best attempts at self-righteousness will fall utterly short: "We have all become like one who is unclean, and all our righteous deeds are like a polluted garment. We all fade like a leaf, and our iniquities, like the wind, take us away" (Isaiah 64:6).

So, we're all in this boat together—and it's the Titanic! Yep, we're sinking fast in the sea of God's judgment and wrath, knowing full well that the iceberg of temptation has penetrated the hull of our ship and now we're filling up fast with the wrath of God. Not one person, from the lowest to the highest, from the least to the greatest are outside the destruction of sin.

So, first, let me tell you, there is not one person better or worse than another before the watching eyes of God. The only difference between a Christian and a person who is lost is that the Christian has come to receive the free gift of God's mercy in Christ Jesus. Consider this truth: the best golfers in the world are only that good because they have taken the time to practice and build their skills until they can withstand the rigors of the courses they play. But they still make mistakes… they still sin. And even the best of Christians will still stumble along the road of life.

Now, second, let me say that you do not have to remain trapped in sin and lost before God. You can get into the lifeboat! The Lord Jesus Christ is waiting to take you from the sinking ship of sin and place you into the security of His grace. Jesus said, "All that the Father gives me will come to me, and whoever comes to me I will never cast out" (John 6:37). Again, the call of the Lord Jesus is clear, "Come to me, all who labor and are heavy laden, and I will give you rest. Take my yoke upon you, and learn from me, for I am gentle and lowly in heart, and you will find rest for your souls" (Matthew 11:28-29).

It's true: I will more than likely never compete in any professional tournament or at a level that the pros enjoy. I don't put the time or the effort into my game. They are better than me in the practical experience of the game. And there are Christians who strive to make their life all that it can be for the Lord. They work and labor and discipline themselves until they have mastered their own passions and solidified the purpose of God in their life. Paul says it like this:

> Do you not know that in a race all the runners run, but only one receives the prize? So run that you may obtain it. Every athlete exercises self-control in all things. They do it to receive a perishable wreath, but we an imperishable. So I do not run aimlessly; I do not box as one beating the air. But I discipline my body and keep it under control, lest after preaching to others I myself should be disqualified. ~ 1 Corinthians 9:24-27

My question to you is this: are you willing to give the Christian life your all? Will you strive to master your passions and center your life on God's purpose? We all stumble in many ways (James 3:2). Will you get back up and set your feet again to walk in the path of Christ?

Yes, all have sinned. However, there is no reason to let your sin destroy you. Get up again if you've fallen. Through personal confession and repentance the Lord will cleanse and renew you. Be the one who does not let sin have mastery over you (Romans 6:12-14)

Don't Give Up... Surrender

Oh, it was a rough day on the course that day. It seemed like every shot I took veered to the right or the left. Trees, hazards, water—even out of bounds all came into play that day... and all with tragic results. I was so frustrated that I was ready to call it done - game over, it's time to quit! No, not just that round. I was ready to give up the game entirely.

Even the great Bobby Jones felt the frustration of the game when, during the Open Championship in 1921, he walked off the Old Course at St. Andrews during the third round.[2]

I think every golfer has experienced that same level of frustration and despair which accompanies a grizzly round of golf. When the entire course is set against you, when every potential birdie becomes a bogey, when you three putt all four-footers and slice every drive into the trees, it seems only fitting that the singular remedy is to abandon the game.

In the round of golf I described above, I was so frustrated that I ended up wrapping my driver around a tree, smashing my wedge into a branch and walking off the course with the intent of never returning again. (I have since repented of that angry outburst.)

But the most debilitating failure of all is the failure that happens when you give up.

And yet, there are many who will abandon their life to the failures of the past. They give up because they believe there is little hope of any victorious life before them. Mistakes of the past have bred a settled despair for the future and shipwrecked

[2] https://en.wikipedia.org/wiki/Old_Course_at_St_Andrews

them on the rocks of disappointment. The hope of having a life restored is lost in the fog of despondency and the only solution they see is to finally give up.

But that is not the solution! The remedy for all such failure is not to give up, it's to surrender. Yes, you read that right. I said surrender.

No, I don't mean for you to surrender to the inevitability of failure, to throw up your hands in frustration and yield to the disappointments. What you and I must do in the days of disaster is to yield all things to Christ, to surrender to the Savior who can take even the most wretched in this world and transform them into a valued and glorious participant in life. Consider the words of Paul:

> The saying is trustworthy and deserving of full acceptance, that Christ Jesus came into the world to save sinners, of whom I am the foremost. But I received mercy for this reason, that in me, as the foremost, Jesus Christ might display his perfect patience as an example to those who were to believe in him for eternal life. To the King of the ages, immortal, invisible, the only God, be honor and glory forever and ever. Amen. ~ 1 Timothy 1:15-17

The problem that many Christians struggle with is the idea that God cannot use someone who has missed the mark. If that's the case, then God cannot use anyone - for, remember, all have sinned. Even the most grievous of sinners can be redeemed. Your opportunities might not be as they would have been before the fact, but it does not mean the situation is hopeless.

Consider this: God called a man to lead the nation of Israel out of slavery – that man was Moses and he was a confirmed murderer. God sought out a man after His own heart to be the king of Israel and the ancestor to the King of kings. That man was David and he was an adulterer. God recruited a man to be the voice of the gospel to the Gentiles. Who did He call? Yes, the Apostle Paul – who was once Saul of Tarsus and was a vicious persecutor of the church. Even the thief on the cross found his moment to be more than all his past could have prevented (see Luke 23:39-43).

Concerning the work of Christ, we close with this thought:

> …who gave himself for us to redeem us from all lawlessness and to purify for himself a people for his own possession who are zealous for good works. ~ Titus 2:14

Christ has redeemed us, made us new. All the failed shots of the past can be forgiven. Consequences may be in play and must be endured, but the next shot you take can be for the glory of Jesus.

Hole Eleven

The Walk

I LOVE NEW courses. Not new in the sense that they were just constructed (okay, that would be fun too), but new in the fact that I have never played on it. And, after moving to the small mountain town where I now reside, there were many courses within driving distance that I had never played.

The course I chose on one particular day was a pristine and beautiful sanctuary. Lush fairways and manicured greens waited like heaven before my eyes. I was young then, younger than I am now, and I loathed taking a riding cart on a golf course. I only needed a pull cart for my bag and I would step out for miles of evergreens, blue skies and the sweet scent of fresh cut grass. Ah, delightful.

Before I continue regaling you with this tale, you need to know a bit of the back-story. In the clubhouse, the course offered a package deal - green fees, lunch and a riding cart all for a reasonable price. However, when I told them I didn't want to take a cart, they looked at me with a puzzled expression. "There's no discount for walking" the clerk clarified for me, but I was still intent on hoofing it around the course.

I waited through the queue of golfers as they rolled their way to the first tee and launched their day into the air. Then it was my turn! I stepped up to the tee box and looked out over a hill that, I believe, fell off the edge of the earth. No matter. I struck my shot straight down the fairway and I was off. But, as I learned that day, what goes downhill must eventually come back up again.

And that was my round. Down and up… up and down. The hills of the course never once flattened out to make the walk any less grueling. There was no end in sight - nothing but high rolling mounds and steep valleys. Like a slow moving rollercoaster, up and down I went. Part of the course might have done a loop-d-loop for all I knew. I endured marches in the military with less difficulty!

At the end of eighteen holes, I was exhausted and sore. Sweat poured from me and I think I drank at least six bottles of water. The best part of my game was between holes five and thirteen: after the shock wore off and before the exhaustion set in. and though I have played that course many times since, I have never walked those eighteen holes again. I learned my lesson. Even now as I look back, I'm glad to say that I did walk it at least once.

So, here I am, several years later and although I take a cart more often than I used to, I still like to walk. There is something tranquil and sublime about the journey around a golf course. Walk the course and you get the opportunity to experience the rigors of the round, the delights of the environment and the joy of spending time nestled in the pageantry of God's creation. When I walk, I keep pace with my own thoughts, and am able to make better shots. I don't rush, but I don't play slow. I enjoy the day more.

There are those who view life as always lived in the "fast lane." They are the ones who rent the carts from the clubhouse and rush along the fairways of life to try and catch up with, well, who knows what. It's as if they view life in fast-forward and never take the time to realize why they're alive in the first place. Then there are others who tend to pace themselves with such measured steps and move so slow that you begin to wonder if they're moving at all.

I'll admit I've been a part of that first category. Life was to be lived—and lived in a hurry! Kids are eager to grow up; teens are quick to try and become adults; and young adults are rushing to get to whatever successes they have imagined. Now, however, I am at a more sensible age and I tend to view life with a bit more serenity. I've slowed down a bit. I don't drive the ball as far, but I hit it with better accuracy. I still walk the course, but do so with a gentler stride. I still play a bit fast (three hours for a round is my average). Yet, now, I am enjoying the journey so much more.

And this is more than just about golf. I'm talking about life.

You might be asking, "What does walking a golf course have to do with Christianity?" Good question.

From the moment you are born again, you are on a journey from here to heaven. You are walking with Jesus along the way and taking steps through this life with purpose. So ask yourself: What will you need to walk the course of life with Jesus?

A Good Pair of Shoes

Have you ever played golf in tennis shoes? How about loafers or dress shoes? I must admit, I can say yes to all of the above. And the truth is: I didn't think it mattered.

In the early days of my acquaintance with golf, when I stepped onto the fairway and walked along with friends who were also just starting out in the game, I never bothered to worry about my footwear. Whatever I showed up in, that's what I wore when I walked the course. It didn't matter if they were tennis shoes, Sunday dress shoes, or even combat boots when I served in the military. Whatever was on my feet is what I wore. I even witnessed a man playing a round of golf wearing flip-flops.

Be that as it may, several years after I had taken up the game, I happened to be on the driving range when the club pro was out teaching a lesson. In all honesty, I scheduled my time to be on the driving range in order to hear the club pro give lessons to someone else because I couldn't afford it myself. Anyway, there I was, striking ball after ball, when the pro came over to me.

"You know," he said, "you'll hit the ball with greater accuracy if you can stabilize your feet. Get yourself a good pair of golf shoes, you won't regret it."

I looked up at him, and then glanced down at my tennis shoes. They were decent shoes, comfortable and good for long walks. He simply smiled and walked away. That may have been the best free coaching I ever received!

The Christian life is a race, a journey, a marathon that will require you to get yourself the right pair of shoes. Consider the words of the Apostle Paul to the church in Ephesus: "…and as shoes for your feet, having put on the readiness given by the gospel of peace" (Ephesians 6:15).

Paul, in this text, is adorning the Christian life in terms of military readiness. And a soldier, with his feet firmly embedded in a pair of shoes made for combat, will be able to stand in the day of battle and endure the rigors of long marches.

For the Christian, then, the "shoes" that you wear must be more than the "slippers" of ease and comfort. They must be more than the "dress shoes" of popularity and prestige. Your Christian footwear must be able to carry you on this journey and keep you ready in the day of difficulty. That, my friends, is the shoes of the gospel.

There are times, I fear, many Christians walk around in spiritual "flip-flops," never embracing more than just a casual acquaintance with the journey they are on. But God has called

His people to be fitted with the shoes of the gospel. What does that mean? Simple: every direction you choose, every step you take, every purpose you endeavor to accomplish is marked by the gospel of Jesus Christ. The believer walks through this life in the confidence of the gospel, knowing that he or she is at peace with God and can stand secure because of the promises God has made in Christ.

Without the gospel of Jesus I have no security, no stability and no means to walk through this world which is filled with the thorns and briers of sin. It is the gospel that crushes all the snares of the enemy and gives me sure footing because I know to Whom I belong. What is the gospel? Paul gives the answer quite clearly:

> Now I would remind you, brothers, of the gospel I preached to you, which you received, in which you stand, and by which you are being saved, if you hold fast to the word I preached to you—unless you believed in vain. For I delivered to you as of first importance what I also received: that Christ died for our sins in accordance with the Scriptures, that he was buried, that he was raised on the third day in accordance with the Scriptures, and that he appeared to Cephas, then to the twelve. Then he appeared to more than

> five hundred brothers at one time, most of whom are still alive, though some have fallen asleep. Then he appeared to James, then to all the apostles. Last of all, as to one untimely born, he appeared also to me. ~ 1 Corinthians 15:1-8

Simply put: Jesus lived the perfect life, died for our sins, rose from the dead three days later, was witnessed by multiple people and now lives in glory as the King of kings and Lord of lords, giving salvation to all who believe. To fit your feet in the shoes of the gospel is to walk through this world with steadfast trust in the Lord Jesus Christ.

Endurance to the End

Sometimes, walking the course is a simple task. With level fairways and no rolling hills or elevations to hike, you find yourself strolling along with ease. Clean, fresh air and beautiful surroundings often make the journey a pleasant and delightful time.

Then there are those "other" courses. You've been on them as well, I know because I can hear the exhaustion in your memories. They are the courses that tax your limits, which strain your muscles and your nerves. There are courses so difficult they can only be walked by mountain goats! More than long, they are arduous, with elevation changes on every hole that would test even the hardiest climber. I played on one course where you needed to hold onto a pulley rope from the green of one hole to the tee box of the next. Yes! It had a motorized pull-rope to help you reach the next level.

If you watch (or play) the professional tours, the courses that they navigate are often a test of endurance as well as shot making ability. No wonder fitness and strength trainers are becoming the norm for tour players – it's needed just to walk the course!

The Christian life is a life of endurance. There are rugged paths to walk, and the Bible makes it clear that the ones who endure show themselves to be followers of Jesus. Our Lord's own word says it clearly, "But the one who endures to the end will be saved" (Matthew 24:13). It is not an easy road, and it never was meant to be. Even the entrance to follow Christ is a narrow one and the road that is described is hard:

> Enter by the narrow gate. For the gate is wide and the way is easy that leads to destruction, and those who enter by it are many. For the gate is narrow and the way is hard that leads to life, and those who find it are few. ~ Matthew 7:13-14

I do not deny that there is a modern trend in Christianity to try and make it appealing to the masses by minimizing the challenge of walking with Jesus. I will not do that here. The road to follow Christ, to walk the fairways with Jesus, is to walk a rugged and challenging road that is filled with difficulty and danger. You will be opposed by the world, regarded as ignorant by some, laughed at and ridiculed by others. As I write this, there have been mass killings of Christians in various parts of the world simply because they claim Jesus as their Savior.

So, let me give you a bit of a warning: if you are being invited to follow Christ and the way they are showing you is wide and the gate to enter is easy, that, my friends, is the wrong road.

But, do not mistake me. To follow Jesus is to walk a life filled with joy, overflowing with purpose, glistening with moments of amazing glory, and empowered to do things given by God and with eternal significance. At the end of the journey is a home waiting for you, not built by human hands, created for all who love and serve the Lord. Consider the words from the book of Hebrews:

> Therefore, since we are surrounded by so great a cloud of witnesses, let us also lay aside every weight, and sin which clings so closely, and let us run with endurance the race that is set before us, looking to Jesus, the founder and perfecter of

> our faith, who for the joy that was set before him endured the cross, despising the shame, and is seated at the right hand of the throne of God. Consider him who endured from sinners such hostility against himself, so that you may not grow weary or fainthearted. ~ Hebrews 12:1-3

How do you run this race? With endurance. By keeping your eyes on Jesus and letting Him set the pace, you will discover a growing strength to carry on until you reach the final hole and step off the course of this life into the glorious home awaiting: Heaven.

Hole Twelve

Course Conditions

YOU PLAY THE course as you find it. This rule (which we will cover in more detail in another chapter) sets the stage for your golfing adventure. And, I must say, I think I've played in almost every condition available. In fact, it takes quite a bit of trouble to get me off the course – lightning strikes will do it every time!

I've played in such thick fog that the moment the ball flew off the clubface it vanished through the curtain of clouds. There have been days when the rains were so hard and the ground soaked that the ball, though hit in the center of the fairway, was

swallowed up by the earth and vanished from view when it plugged in the wet sod. Sweltering heat is a common occurrence, for most golf is played in the summer.
But I have played golf when the ground was frozen and the ball bounced off the green like it had landed on concrete. I've played in snow, hail, sleet, and wind. There's no escaping this truth: if you're serious about playing golf, then you will play in almost any condition.

And, perhaps, that is one of the tests that mark the difference between the serious player and the casual participant of the game. I have no trouble with the casual participant, and I enjoy their company when the course is crowded. They tend toward the jovial, and often bring a bit of humor to the round. Sometimes they lark about, but usually they navigate the course with a carefree disposition that can be refreshing. But they're found on the course usually when it's sunny and warm, with gentle breezes and kindly conditions. You'll never see the causal golfer on the course when it's raining.

For the Christian, the conditions of this world are ever changing. There are days when the weather's fair, when life is at ease and the way is clear. And then there are times when the world has risen against the believer, turning the conditions harsh and hard. Such was the situation of one young Christian in the Book of Acts, a believer by the name of: John Mark.

Now, there's not much said about him in consideration of this idea of the conditions of our world, but knowing what he does brings us to a place of recognition. Let's look at three passages:

> And Barnabas and Saul Returned from Jerusalem when they had completed their service, bringing with them John, whose other name was Mark. ~ Acts 12:25
>
> Now Paul [formerly Saul] and his companions set sail from Paphos and came to Perga in Pamphylia. And John left them and returned to Jerusalem. ~ Acts 13:13
>
> And after some days Paul said to Barnabas, "Let us return and visit the brothers in every city where we proclaimed the word of the Lord, and see how they are." Now Barnabas wanted to take with them John called Mark. But Paul thought best not to take with them one who had withdrawn from them in Pamphylia and had not gone with them to the work. And there arose a sharp disagreement, so that they separated from each other. Barnabas took Mark with him and sailed away to Cyprus, but Paul chose Silas and departed, having been commended by the brothers to the grace of the Lord. And he went through Syria and Cilicia, strengthening the churches. ~ Acts 15:36-41

What happened? Why did John Mark depart and no longer travel with the group once they reached Pamphylia? Based on what happens to Paul and Barnabas after he leaves, it appears that John Mark abandoned the work for fear of the hostility and persecution they suffered. The conditions changed, and the way of following Christ became far more difficult. But, in light of the rest of the story, John Mark learned how to endure the rigors of hostile conditions and even found his way back into the heart of the Apostle, for Paul referenced him in his final letter: "Luke alone is with me. Get Mark and bring him with you, for he is very useful to me for ministry" (2 Timothy 4:11).

Conditions weed out the Causal Participant

My son is a passionate golfer. I would say he's even more addicted to the sport than I am. He doesn't tend to watch it so much, but when the moment comes for him to step out on the fairway, he is all over it. I learned this about him when we first went out to the course together.

For about a year I had been practicing almost every day. After work I would drive to the local course and putt on the practice greens and hit chips and short irons in a narrow field alongside the course. The manager didn't mind so much as I was always there to play every week as well. That year I began teaching my youngest son the game. We'd swing clubs in the yard and practice putting in the house. Every time he would beg me to take him out to the golf course till finally, on this one particular day, I did.

The weather in Washington can change throughout the day, and though it started with clear skies, that's not how it ended. By the third hole, the wind began to pick up and the temperature started dropping. I asked him if he wanted to call it quits. "No dad," he said, and hit his next shot. We turn the corner and a drizzling rain fell, causing the air to grow chill. Both of us donned our windbreakers and, with a nod from my son, we pressed on.

By the fifteenth hole, his teeth were chattering. He changed gloves a couple of times because of how wet it was, and then the weather got worse. Hail began to fall. Dark clouds filled the sky and with them, that ominous sense of dread. At this point I was ready to pack it in, until I looked in my son's eyes. I had never seen such a brighter look of happiness. He was practically beaming with joy and no amount of weather would steal his first round of golf. I knew then, he was hooked.

Golfers scurried off the course, heads hung against the blowing rain. Others drove off, quickly following the cart path to the sanctuary of the clubhouse. Soon we were alone, soaked to the bone, and shivering with delight. By the time we returned to the clubhouse, having completed the entire eighteen holes, no other cars remained in the parking lot except those who worked there. Large cups of hot cocoa were the order of the moment and we sipped at the warmth with gladness.

A standing theme throughout the Scriptures is the reality of the casual observer versus the dedicated follower. Often during His ministry on earth Jesus had thousands following Him, receiving the benefit of His presence and watching His work. They seemed eager to connect with the Savior, but only so long as He continued to pour out His blessings and miracles upon them. When the way became difficult and the teaching became hard, they left the course. Consider what happens in John chapter six:

> When many of his disciples heard it, they said, "This is a hard saying; who can listen to it?" But Jesus, knowing in himself that his disciples were grumbling about this, said to them, "Do you take offense at this? Then what if you were to see the Son of Man ascending to where he was before? It is the Spirit who gives life; the flesh is no help at all. The words that I have spoken to you are spirit and life. But there are some of you who do not believe." (For Jesus knew from the beginning who those were who did not believe, and who it was who would betray him.) And he said, "This is why I told you that no one can come to me unless it is granted him by the Father." After this many of his disciples turned back and no longer walked with him. ~ John 6:60-66

This encounter between Jesus and those who seemed to follow Him came just one day after He fed over 5000 of them. But Jesus knew their hearts and told them the reason they followed: "Jesus answered them, 'Truly, truly, I say to you, you are seeking me, not because you saw signs, but because you ate your fill of the loaves'" (v. 26). They were merely casual observers of Jesus, receiving His benefits without dedicating themselves to Him. Such is the casual Christian today.

I have seen many so-called believers fill the halls of the sanctuaries of faith as long as it's comfortable, convenient and care-free. Once the preaching against sin and the call to a dedicated life for Christ begins, these same self-satisfied believers will pull out and find an easier course. So the words of 1 John come to mind, "They went out from us, but they were not of us; for if they had been of us, they would have continued with us. But they went out, that it might become plain that they all are not of us" (1 John 2:19).

It is possible, even as we observed with John Mark, that these casual Christians can find the strength and grace to endure real Christianity and move from casual to committed. Luke 9:23 tells us how, "And he said to all, "If anyone would come after me, let him deny himself and take up his cross daily and follow me."

Conditions Test Your Mettle more than Your Skill

The other thing that course conditions will do is test your mettle - even more than your skills. A golf shot is a golf shot and if you're a hack golfer in fair weather you'll be the same in foul weather too. If you have skills and can navigate a course with some precision, then you will adjust to the conditions and press on. Certainly the score will often reflect the conditions you play in, but the hardiness of a player is tested in the environment they must endure.

As you may have guessed, I am an avid golfer. I actually used to be fairly good. Though my skills have diminished over time, my love for the game has never waned. I keep my clubs in the car year round and would take them with me as I speak around the country if the cost of baggage on airlines wasn't so high. But, they have rental clubs at most courses and I will use them when needed. Even now, as I'm writing this, it is a force of will to keep on working and not jump in the car and head out to the nearest course!

And it doesn't much matter what the weather's like - provided there is no lightning and the course is open. I will play a round of golf through it all. But that wasn't always the case.

When I first entered into the strange and surreal world of golfing, I was reluctant - even unwilling - to participate unless it was dry, warm, clear and there was a cart to ride in. Even then, a few bad shots and I found myself ready to abandon ship and go home. As I matured, moving from my teenage years to adulthood, I discovered a growing endurance and resolve to press on. I found a fortitude within me that changed the way I played the game. It was no longer a trivial experience with no value; golf became for me a proving ground of mental and physical consistency. And now, I truly admire those who play four-day tournaments on very difficult courses. They walk for at least four hours each day and must maintain mental focus through all manner of conditions and difficulties. And, unlike many other sports, golf does not test you against another player—golf tests you against yourself.

The Christian life truly pits you against yourself. Yes, there is an enemy that lurks in the shadows of life, tempting and

persecuting the church, causing havoc and mayhem as much as possible. But the truth is, as a Christian, you possess a power to endure far greater than you might realize. The conditions around you, whether hardships or sufferings or persecutions or temptations, will test your mettle and your willingness to endure for Christ's sake.
James clearly identifies these difficulties as the "testing of your faith."

> Count it all joy, my brothers, when you meet trials of various kinds, for you know that the testing of your faith produces steadfastness. And let steadfastness have its full effect, that you may be perfect and complete, lacking in nothing. ~ James 1:2-4

Some of the greatest and most courageous among us are the soldiers who stand as the wall of defense around our country. And though I played a small part in my time with the U.S. Air Force, I am honored to have been numbered among them. The valiant courage displayed by our soldiers and the will to endure that marks their lives gives a powerful illustration to the endurance that God calls His people to display. Paul tells his young disciple, Timothy, to endure hardship as a good soldier of Jesus (2 Timothy 2:3).

Consider this quick assessment from the Apostle Paul concerning his own life and ministry:

> We put no obstacle in anyone's way, so that no fault may be found with our ministry, but as servants of God we commend ourselves in every way: by great endurance, in afflictions, hardships, calamities, beatings, imprisonments, riots, labors, sleepless nights, hunger; by purity, knowledge, patience, kindness, the Holy Spirit, genuine love; by truthful speech, and the power of God; with the weapons of righteousness for the right hand and for the left; through honor and dishonor, through slander and praise. We are treated as impostors, and yet are true; as unknown, and yet well known; as dying, and behold, we live; as punished, and yet not killed; as sorrowful, yet always rejoicing; as poor, yet making many rich; as having nothing, yet possessing everything. ~ 2 Corinthians 6:3-10

Light or heavy, easy or hard, the way before you is marked by both. The question never is whether one or the other is agreeable to you, but whether or not you will walk the path before you no matter the conditions of the course.

Hole Thirteen

The Caddie

IT IS DEEPLY satisfying when you experience great victories because of successful partnerships. History is filled with such collaborations and many find that in working together they can accomplish exponentially more than they would have alone. Some examples would be: Orville and Wilbur Wright who developed the mechanism that made fixed-wing flight a possibility, Drs. Francis Crick and James Watson who unlocked the informational code known as DNA, and, despite the modern legendary myth that Al Gore invented the internet, credit goes to Larry Page and Sergey Brin who brought the world to our laptops.

Ancient and modern legends carry the sense of comradery with the stories of such heroes as Batman and Robin, The Lone Ranger and Tonto, Han Solo and Chewbacca, Kirk, Spock and McCoy (Yes… Star Trek), Sherlock Holmes and Dr. Watson… and we must not forget Frodo and Sam!

Golf, also, has its dynamic duos. Of course there is Mickelson and Mackay who will go down in golf history as one of the best pro/caddie tandems in the sport. Tom Watson and Bruce Edwards are forever etched in the annals of legendary duos. Throughout the history of the game, golfers have found great success with a trusted caddie on the bag, and those stories will continue as long as golf is played. There is a tremendous advantage to such partnerships, not least of which is the encouragement that comes from knowing someone stands beside you through all the trials and triumphs that are experienced in the game.

Even a quick glance through the Word of God and you will discover friendships and comraderies of such value that the very work of God is accomplished because of it. Men like Moses, whom God called to lead the people of Israel, needed someone who stood beside him and be a part of the work. So

God sent Aaron, his brother, to be that joint-laborer (Exodus 4). Deborah, in her fight against the armies that came against Israel called upon Barak and found in him a much needed ally (Judges 4). Jonathan and his armor bearer stood together and routed a garrison of the Philistines (1 Samuel 14).

And the list would go on and on. Read through the Book of Acts and you happen upon men like Peter and John standing boldly before the Sanhedrin or Paul and Silas encouraging one another in a Philippian jail. All throughout the ages such friendships and fellowships of men and women have been the backbone of the church, adding strength and encouragement to one another.

There is tremendous value in a shared adventure. I remember a time when I played alongside a friend and I hit a chip-in eagle on a par five. I found tremendous joy in sharing that flash of triumph with someone who knew the value of the game. It was as if I had more than doubled the joy of that moment because of having someone along. Another moment came for me once, when, from the fairway - about 150 yards out - I hit another great shot and it rolled in the cup for an eagle! Par four in two, and as I rejoiced in great celebration, it felt almost empty for not having anyone there to share it. We need companionship in life - a caddie who will help us navigate the road.

A Partner will Multiply Your Strength

I've only used a caddie once in my experience as a golfer. Now, that's not to say that I haven't conscripted my son into caddie duties when I've been on the course. But the purpose of that was to show him how to read greens, select clubs and make his own way around. It thrilled my heart the moment I lined up a putt and he correctly pointed out the break and speed of the green. Since then, however, he's been my playing partner—not my caddie.

Anyway, I have used an actual caddie once. It was on a private course that a friend had invited me to play. He and I, along with one other person, entered the clubhouse to pay for our round. Okay, he paid for it - a gift to me and my friend for helping him through a difficult time. So, there at the counter, I asked for a pull-cart for my bag. The look on the face of the clerk was priceless! It was as if I had asked if I could please take a garden trowel and carve my initials on every fairway. "Oh, sir," said the man behind the counter, "we don't use pull-carts here." Yep… I felt like the Clampetts in Beverly Hills! And, if you know that reference, you know what I mean.

So, there I was, without a pull-cart and imagining myself lugging my clubs for eighteen holes. And my friend who invited me to the course simply smiled like the Cheshire Cat as we walked to the first tee. Waiting at the tee box stood two young men, older teens to be exact, and they had no clubs to speak of. I glanced at the man who paid for the round and he smiled and said, "Yes… these are the caddies."

It was a delightful time after that. My caddie was very knowledgeable about the course, instructed about the game and rules, and adept at helping me find my way along. He pulled clubs for me, suggested types of shots (flops, fades, chips and so on). All-in-all, he became a valued addition to my game. In fact, I would have to admit, that I enjoyed the game so much more with a companion on the journey. He added a new viewpoint and a set of skills that improved my game. He helped me avoid hazards, read greens and even find the ball when it was lost in the woods.

But that is the joy of having a person with you who is a part of the process of success. They multiply your strength, bring a fresh and new perspective, help with skills that you may not possess and provide valued counsel to navigate the hazards along the way.

Consider what it says in Ecclesiastes about having a comrade-in-arms:

> Two are better than one, because they have a good reward for their toil. For if they fall, one

> will lift up his fellow. But woe to him who is alone when he falls and has not another to lift him up! Again, if two lie together, they keep warm, but how can one keep warm alone? And though a man might prevail against one who is alone, two will withstand him—a threefold cord is not quickly broken. ~ Ecclesiastes 4:9-12

But that is the Christian life! We do not labor and work alone. Through the church, Christians will find strength and support for the work that God has called them to do. According to the previous text, two have a multiplying effect in their labor. With a partner along the journey, if one falls, the other can render the needed aid. There is shared comfort in the cold climate of a hostile environment to the Gospel. There is added protection when the adversaries of Christ strike against the believer. Everything you need to fulfill your work in Christ will not be found exclusively through you. The church is designed to work in cooperation with one another so that the effort is multiplied.

I remember a time when, while serving in the U.S. Air Force in South Korea, a friend and I were sharing the Gospel downtown in the city where we lived. Andy was his name, and he and I would walk the streets talking to anyone who spoke English about the Lord Jesus Christ.

We had a marvelous partnership and friendship. He possessed an uncanny ability to open up conversations with total strangers as if they were old acquaintances. At the time, I was far more reserved - shy, to put it mildly - and trembled at the idea of opening up a dialogue with someone I didn't know. As Andy turned the conversation to spiritual matters, he would get bogged down in the issues of Scripture - and that's where I came in. I come alive when talking about Jesus and the Lord has blessed me to be able to share His Word.

So, when questions came up that were beyond his reach, I answered and spoke and eventually gathered a crowd around who would listen. Together, Andy and I were wonderfully blessed to work side-by-side and we witnessed many people come to Christ. We needed each other and multiplied the labor because of the gifts and skills we brought to work. Even now, as I think about it, I would love to find another "Andy" to partner with in the cause of Christ.

A Partner will Magnify Your Support

It was a rough day on the course that day. Every shot went awry. Slices, hooks, pulls, pushes—and that was just my putting stroke! On a beautiful summer day, my head was covered by the dark cloud of grim reality. My game had fallen apart.

But then there was my playing partner that day. He was another pastor, a friend and co-laborer with Christ. And his game was even worse. He drove the ball from the tee and worms would jump out of the way. His divots flew farther than his ball and four putts were a thing of common occurrence. I'm not sure if even one chip shot held the green and yet he possessed a joy that seemed unbreakable.

After the devastating reality of another horrific shot, as my temper began to burn like a magma beneath a volcano, my friend looked at me with a whimsical smile and said, "Michael… it's just a game." His tone of voice, the look in his eye, everything about him in that moment diffused a potential explosion. He wasn't condescending; he didn't laugh at my shots or poke fun at my anger. He spoke with a light-heartedness that was exactly the right temperature to cool my internal rage.

Not surprising to any of you who play golf, the moment my internal fury had subsided, my game improved dramatically.

There is something special about having a friend along for the ride, one who can bring a settled peace and more centered focus to the journey. Good caddies, those who stay with their golfers for a long time, can build healthy relationships which may bring about a calm and focused outlook on the game. And good friends, who travel with you on the path of faith, will do that and more.

Romans 15:2 states: "Let each of us please his neighbor for his good, to build him up." That's the goal – to build each other up in the faith. Again, in 1 Thessalonians 5:11, "Therefore encourage one another and build one another up, just as you are doing." It is so important that, as Christians, we strive to help each other along the pathway of faith. Without mutual support and encouragement, many will be cast upon the road of despair without anyone to pick them up.

Many often use Hebrews 10:24-25 as a reminder to continue gathering with the church, and for good reason. It is in the fellowship of God's people that there is a magnified support: "And let us consider how to stir up one another to love and good works, not neglecting to meet together, as is the habit of some, but encouraging one another, and all the more as you see the Day drawing near."

The command in the previous text truly means to "prod them toward love and good works." How is this accomplished? Simple – do not neglect meeting together and encourage one another. So, basically: "Get together and lift each other up." And do this "all the more" because that day is coming when Christ will return and all our labors will be ended. The caddie need not encourage the player when the game is over. But there is a great need for encouragement when the game is being played. There will be no need for mutual encouragement in Heaven. It is only on the battle field, in the midst of the struggle, when mutual encouragement and support are in desperate need.

So, who's your caddie? I have very few - and so do you. These are the people allowed into the inner sanctuary of our hearts. It's not everyone - not even everyone in church. Yes, all believers can be mutually encouraging, but those whom we allow to draw closest to us will be the ones who uplift us in those times of strife, who encourage us through our darkest nights, who walk with us along the journey and help us when we collapse from the weight of our lives.

Who do you caddie for? Yes, you're not just the player of your life; you are also the caddie for someone else. Are you close to the heart of anyone so that you can offer more than advice or opinion? Do you have a person or a few people who can rely on you in the days of their darkness, when the time of hardships fall and the road is rough? Do not be so self-focused that God cannot use you to build up the life of another believer. There is joy in the adventure - but let that adventure be shared.

Hole Fourteen

Practice

YOU'VE HEARD THE adage: "Practice makes perfect." Well, if practice made perfect, there would be an overwhelming influx of perfect golfers throughout our land. Every time I go to the golf course I am always amazed at how many are on the driving range, chipping green and practice bunkers working on various aspects of their game.

I noticed one particular golfer on the driving range as I pulled up on a sunny Tuesday morning. He had a large bucket of range balls all spilled out near his feet. As I shuffled past the range, he had driver in hand and thwack! His ball sailed high and right - very right in fact. It sailed right into the adjoining fairway. His frustration was palpable. He teed up another and… thwack. Yep, it went high and right. Each shot, time and time again, faced the same dismal result.

The man would look at his club, pondering the item as if it contained some horrendous flaw. He banged it on the ground with each shot demanding compliance from the device. Occasionally he would raise his hands in anguished despair. The one thing he never tried to do, as I watched this episode of futility unfold, he never tried to change his swing. No adjustment, no imaginative reworking of his swing plane, he didn't even re-adjust his grip. One bad shot followed another and then he started walking toward the first tee, his round soon underway.

I can only imagine how his round played out. He was in the group behind me and I never did see his first tee shot, but the time he spent in practice could not have translated into a good game.

I recall, somewhere in the vast echo-chamber of my memory, having heard that the definition of insanity is to do the same thing over and over again and expect different results. Perhaps it's correct, or perhaps there is a deeper reality to the condition of insanity, but, I am convinced, that golfer who left the driving range was certain to be out of his mind by the end of his round.

There are Christians who take their walk with Christ the same as that golfer on the range. What I mean is this: Christians across the land look at everything outside themselves to try and determine the reasons their faith is in chaos, their walk is more of a crawl and their life in Christ lacks all the power, presence and purpose that is promised in the Word of God.

Some will look at the church, pondering the fellowship with a jaundiced eye, thinking that it must be the church or the pastor at fault for their failed faith. I served in a church that had three sister churches nearby. Invariably, almost every three months, there would be a "rotation" of believers from one church to another. This group would be offended at something (even as insignificant as the carpet color) and move to the next church. This went on for the time I served there and I never noticed any of those believers actually maturing in their faith.

Others will shake their fists at something as trivial as the style of music, pounding it with their opinions in hopes of demanding compliance. They can't stand hymns or they despise modern Christian music. The sermons are too long or too short (actually, I've never heard that latter complaint). I suppose there are some who just cannot grow without PowerPoint and massive stage presentations. Any way you slice it (yes… pun intended), people will first look outside themselves to determine the cause of their failure.

But the human condition is such that we are embattled within. The fight against maturity in Christ comes not from external circumstances but from internal corruption. The world and all its conditions cannot prevent you from growing in the faith and the life of Christ. Just like the golfer on the driving range – it was not the club, the ball, the tee or the environment that hindered him, it was himself.

Consider the words of the Apostle Paul:

> For we know that the law is spiritual, but I am of the flesh, sold under sin. For I do not understand my own actions. For I do not do what I want, but I do the very thing I hate. Now if I do what I do not want, I agree with the law, that it is good. So now it is no longer I who do it, but sin that dwells within me. For I know that nothing good dwells in me, that is, in my flesh. For I have the desire to do what is right, but not the ability to carry it out. For I do not do the good I want, but the evil I do not want is what I keep on doing.

> Now if I do what I do not want, it is no longer I who do it, but sin that dwells within me. ~ Romans 7:14-20

Rethink that statement of Paul: "For I have the desire to do what is right, but not the ability to carry it out." This is the problem with every person who steps onto the course of life with Christ. That man at the driving range had the desire to hit great shots, to sail them straight and long. His desire was admirable, but he did not have the ability.

There are Christians with the desire to do right, to carry out God's great purpose, but lack the ability because they fail to look within for the hindrances. If all you and I ever do is blame our external circumstances for our failed faith, we will never step out in victory with Christ.

So, practice does not make perfect, but practice is a necessity if anyone is ever going to improve. So, what is a Christian to do? Two things: listen to the right coach and practice the right things.

Listen to the Right Coach

Oh, the infomercials! Those infamous, insipid, sometimes infuriating messages that are meant to inspire and instruct and do little to inform. You've watched them and so have I. Under the cover of darkness, after a particularly grueling day on the golf course, you stay up late into the night and for the next 30 minutes are pelted with a barrage of quick-fix solutions to your swing. Your hand trembles as you reach for the phone. Will your spouse forgive you? The message sounds so convincing. The pitchman is so honest. Each of the players that dance across the screen talks of such amazing results and there's even a professional golfer's endorsement! It's everything you ever dreamed of and all for $39.95.

Yes, it's true, I have in my closet half-a-dozen "infomercials" now broken and battered and I am no better a golfer for trying them. Putting helps and driving aids, videos and swing testers, there are as many external devices to try and fix your game as there are problems in your game. With the promise of greater length off the tee, straighter shots into the fairway, better results around the green, sweeter strokes from the bunker and a host of other assurances that left me hanging my head in despair, what I lacked was a coach.

It is so powerfully important to have a set of eyes watching how you play. I signed on to a local tournament and I was paired with a man who was very good. It was a stroke tournament, raising money for a particular cause. The man was making pars and birdies as I was making bogies and pars. As we turned the corner and prepared to tee off on the tenth hole, we had a moment to wait for the green to clear. He was a kind man and told me: "I've been watching your swing and I think I can fix something. Can I point it out to you?"

I was eager to have his input! He had me swing a few times and then stepped up to me and adjusted my grip and the position of my feet. I put his coaching to the test and the next nine holes were some of the best I had played up to that time. There is no infomercial that can fix what they cannot see. It takes the right coach and a willingness to listen.

And, as there is a right coach, I want to first warn you against listening to the wrong one. Paul was greatly concerned about the local church in Galatia. Some had infiltrated their ranks and began teaching a doctrine and faith that was inconsistent to the truth.

> You were running well. Who hindered you from obeying the truth? This persuasion is not from him who calls you. A little leaven leavens the whole lump. I have confidence in the Lord that you will take no other view, and the one who is troubling you will bear the penalty, whoever he is. ~ Galatians 5:7-10

Peter warns the church that there will be those who bring false teachings into the fellowship: "But false prophets also arose among the people, just as there will be false teachers among you, who will secretly bring in destructive heresies, even denying the Master who bought them, bringing upon themselves swift destruction" (2 Peter 2:1).

You need to listen to the right coach. And the first right coach for the Christian is the Holy Spirit through the Word of God. Jesus promised that the Spirit will guide us into all truth (John 16:13). It is the Holy Spirit who brings about the inner conviction and transformation of the life. Jesus said of the Holy Spirit, "And when he comes, he will convict the world concerning sin and righteousness and judgment" (John 16:8). Paul brings the work of the Holy Spirit to light in 1 Corinthians.

> For who knows a person's thoughts except the spirit of that person, which is in him? So also no one comprehends the thoughts of God except the Spirit of God. Now we have received not the spirit of the world, but the Spirit who is from God, that we might understand the things freely given us by God. And we impart this in words not taught by human wisdom but taught by the Spirit, interpreting spiritual truths to those who are spiritual. ~ 1 Corinthians 2:11-13

And, when the Spirit interacts in the heart it does so with the power of God's word. Hebrews 4:12-13 declare, "For the word of God is living and active, sharper than any two-edged sword, piercing to the division of soul and of spirit, of joints and of marrow, and discerning the thoughts and intentions of the heart. And no creature is hidden from his sight, but all are naked and exposed to the eyes of him to whom we must give account."

You must listen to the right coach, for the world will saturate you with the "infomercials" of self-improvement that do not conform to the word of God or lead you to a more holy life in Christ.

Practice the Right Things

Now comes time to practice. The fact is, without practice there will never be improvement - but you must practice the right things.

I have noticed that there is a problem in my swing. I am a "caster" of the club, which causes me to invariably slice the ball. Now, I could try and play this on every hole and hope for the best, or I can try and make tough corrections until a better swing path is developed. But my first question was: where did this bad habit come from? Easy: it came from bad practice.

Several years ago I injured myself helping a woman move her van from the drive-thru at a local KFC. Two ribs were dislocated and I was laid up for nearly a year in pain. Guess what happened to my game? Yep, it fell to pieces. When I returned to the game I had lost all my distance and my accuracy took a "variable-trajectory" approach. That is to say, I was spraying the ball all over the course - and rarely on the fairway. I was still sore and developed a swing path that felt comfortable and easy to use. However, it also was an out-to-in casting of the club that eliminated any hope of a good shot. That swing plane was grooved in, and because it was comfortable it was easy to think that I was swinging correctly.

Having finally realized my error, I now taking pains to re-learn a correct swing path and have started to hit the ball with greater skill. But because I had grooved in a faulty swing, when I'm tired or sore I find that I revert back to that old, bad habit. It takes a concerted effort to mentally work on the right swing. But, just yesterday (at the time of this writing) I went out to a local course and, for the first time, played a round of golf without falling back into the old habit! Practicing the right thing does pay off in time.

Hear the words of Jesus, "Truly, truly, I say to you, everyone who practices sin is a slave to sin" (John 8:34). Have you grown so comfortable with a faulty life that it's simply easier to remain in the habit of sin than to strive to make a change in your life? To practice something is to participate in it in a habitual way – to groove it into your heart and soul so that it becomes a part of your regular routine. And, because we are sinful by nature, the practice of sin feels comfortable.

Peter gives us a list of things to practice, habits that we must add to our faith in order to have an effective and fruitful life in Christ:

> For this very reason, make every effort to supplement your faith with virtue, and virtue with knowledge, and knowledge with self-control, and self-control with steadfastness, and steadfastness with godliness, and godliness with brotherly affection, and brotherly affection with love. For if these qualities are yours and are increasing, they keep you from being ineffective or unfruitful in the knowledge of our Lord Jesus Christ. For whoever lacks these qualities is so nearsighted that he is blind, having forgotten that he was cleansed from his former sins. Therefore, brothers, be all the more diligent to confirm your calling and election, for if you practice these qualities you will never fall. ~ 2 Peter 1:5-10

Paul instructs Timothy to practice the virtues he has commended, "Practice these things, immerse yourself in them, so that all may see your progress" (1 Timothy 4:15).

Hebrews tells us that the mature in Christ are trained through practice: "But solid food is for the mature, for those who have their powers of discernment trained by constant practice to distinguish good from evil" (Hebrews 5:14).

John tells us that one of the evidences of a person being born-again is that they practice righteousness, "If you know that he is righteous, you may be sure that everyone who practices righteousness has been born of him" (1 John 2:29).

Have you worked into your life a habit of sin, a practice of unrighteousness that is keeping you from the life that God has purposed for you? You have to break the habit by working out all that God has worked in (Philippians 2:12-13). You have to train yourself to be godly: "Have nothing to do with irreverent, silly myths. Rather train yourself for godliness; for while bodily training is of some value, godliness is of value in every way, as it holds promise for the present life and also for the life to come" (1 Timothy 4:7-8). It will take the discipline of effort and faith to do what God wants. But you cannot say you have faith in Christ if you're unwilling to put into practice those things which will develop the character and virtue of Christ in your life.

God, through the Holy Spirit, is your life coach. The word of God is the instruction. It will take practice - the right kind of practice - to see the necessary changes in order to make your life effective and fruitful for the glory of Christ.

Hole Fifteen

The Rules

IN ANY COMPETITIVE situation, there are rules to govern play. As of this writing, from all that I can gather, there are thirty-four rules of golf with multiple sub-rules—and sub, sub rules—that help to keep the game fair and competitive for all who participate. The USGA (United States Golf Association) and R&A (Royal and Ancient) publish a book called Decisions on the Rules of Golf, a pertinent (if not exciting) read for anyone who is serious about playing the game.

I often head to the golf course with little in mind but to join up with a small band of happy adventurers who are willing to take on one extra person in their group. Sometimes (actually, often) I arrive and there are few who are playing and I just work my way around the course alone. But occasionally I find a bottle-neck of golfers waiting to tee off and I just slip in with a group. On one particularly crowded day on the course, this was exactly the case.

Now, before I go much further with this story, I learned a lesson several years ago that, unless you bring your own foursome to the course, you must be willing to accept a wide variety of personalities and various takes on the game. I've golfed with the business man who uses golf as the method of connecting with potential clients. I've stepped off the tee with the weekender who fancied himself a golf instructor (though he never did hit the ball straight). I've enjoyed rounds with Christians and non-Christians alike and find a wealth of conversations to while away the time from one shot to the next.

However, on this particularly crowded day, I had the dubious privilege to play with a man who was the "rule-keeper." You know the one, the man who kept the rules not only in his head but also in his golf bag. On every hole, with almost every shot, he pulled out his reference book and made sure that I towed the line. It reminded me of a commercial with legendary golfer

Phil Mickelson who peeked out from behind trees and acted as the conscience for the golfer in question. Still today, I have no recollection of what they were selling, but I always remember the image of him popping out from behind a tree every time I find myself playing from the woods.

Anyway, I was playing the round with this man who finally asked me, "Don't you care about the rules?" Of course I do, it's an unfair game if you don't. The rules are put in place to help govern the circumstances between two players. In fact, every society that has two or more people in it will invariably have to come up with some form of law, rule or code of conduct to make sure everything is kept in order. But I told him, as I'll tell you now, the rules are simple – it's us who make them complicated. I discovered, long ago, that if I kept the rules of golf down to their simplest form, I rarely violate them. And for me, the simplest rules of golf are:

1. Play the ball where it lies.

2. Play the course as you find it.

And, it seems to me, many rules made for the game of golf find their fulfillment in these two simple statements.

But the way of humanity is often to complicate the matter. Rulings are made to govern the rules that are already in place.

And in those various rulings some must express their views and establish their own rulings on the rulings that help to manage the rules. (Have I complicated the idea enough?)

For an example - the Lord gave us the Ten Commandments, His rules to govern the human race. The Pharisees took Commandment number four (The Sabbath) and established hundreds upon hundreds of qualifications and stipulations to help clarify the rule of God. In essence, they made thousands of sub-rules to try and clarify God's instruction. But simplicity is what brings clarity; complexity breeds confusion. And that is what the Pharisees ultimately did - they bred confusion.

However - and this is a BIG however - Jesus simplified! He took the Ten Commandments and boiled them down to two.

> But when the Pharisees heard that he had silenced the Sadducees, they gathered together. And one of them, a lawyer, asked him a question to test him. "Teacher, which is the great commandment in the Law?" And he said to him, "You shall love the Lord your God with all your heart and with all your soul and with all your mind. This is the great and first commandment. And a second is like it: You shall love your neighbor as yourself. On these two

> commandments depend all the Law and the Prophets." ~ Matthew 22:34-40

That's it... just two.

1. Love the Lord your God with all that you are.

2. Love your neighbor as you love yourself.

If you and I could take our lives and boil our rules down to their bare elements, what would they be?

The Solid Foundation

There is something structurally sound about a solid foundation. Everything built on it has the advantage of stability and strength. And the first thing you build is a solid foundation. Have you ever seen a high-rise structure being built from the top down? Of course not. It always begins with a solid foundation, a sure place to stand.

But what does a solid foundation have to do with the rules? Consider, for a moment, a tournament without rules to govern play. Everyone come into the game with their own ideas, their own rules, their own method of gauging whether or not they won. The tournament would end in chaos and, perhaps, not even take flight at all. The governing laws established by the authorities in charge are meant to give equal footing to all who participate in the activity. And everyone who participates in the games must submit to the rules or be disqualified.

Even the Apostle Paul recognized this simple truth: "An athlete is not crowned unless he competes according to the rules" (2 Timothy 2:5). In the context of this passage, Paul was encouraging his young disciple, Timothy, to make sure that he serves according to the word of God.

And a life cannot be built without the solid foundation of the word of God.

Jesus declared this important truth with the illustration of building a house on either solid ground or shifting sand:

> "Everyone then who hears these words of mine and does them will be like a wise man who built his house on the rock. And the rain fell, and the floods came, and the winds blew and beat on that house, but it did not fall, because it had been founded on the rock. And everyone who hears these words of mine and does not do them will be like a foolish man who built his house on the sand. And the rain fell, and the floods came, and the winds blew and beat against that house, and it fell, and great was the fall of it." ~ Matthew 7:24-27

Diligently pursue the word of God for the sake of obedience, for by it you are standing on and building upon a solid foundation for life.

The Qualifying Rules

In every professional tournament there are some qualifiers that must be met. You have to play a qualifying round or have standing on the PGA, be invited because of certain qualification and so on. Even to play in the qualifying round, there are qualifications to meet. I know this because I read them, to the dismay of my own heart. Yes, I had hoped that my minimal skills at golf might be enough, but I would never have even made it on the course - let alone play in a tournament.

And, briefly, there are some qualifying rules before you are permitted to play the course of the Christian life. Yes… it's not for everyone, but only for those who stand up to the qualifications. To keep it simple, I want to give you the three "R's". No, not "reading, writing and arithmetic" (which is only, actually, one "R"). The three qualifying "R's" for entrance into the Christian life are: "Repent, Return and Respond."

We covered this briefly on Hole Three - The Rough. But to bring it to light further, I want to ask if you have actually done these three things. Paul mentioned these in Acts 26:20, "…but declared first to those in Damascus, then in Jerusalem and throughout all the region of Judea, and also to the Gentiles, that they should repent and turn to God, performing deeds in keeping with their repentance." Have you repented of the rebellion against God that all men are in? Have you received God's grace and mercy and returned to Him through Jesus Christ the Lord? Have you responded to His grace with loving obedience to His word? If you qualify here, then the rules become simple: love God, and love your neighbor.

The Clarity of Simplicity

When I first stepped onto the golf course with my dad, I was inundated with the various rules of the game. He wanted to make sure I understood all the infractions I had committed, trying to correct my approach to the game with an overwhelming infusion of rules. Yes, you guessed it; the joy of the game came to a screeching halt. Golf became for me nothing more than an amalgam of confusing rules and regulations.

To help you understand my dad, he was a correctional officer – a man whose job was to control a society of men behind bars who suffered the stern judgment of the law. His life was about the rules. Stern, harsh at times, golf had rules and abiding by them was paramount.

However, when I began to teach my son the game of golf, I took a different tact. I didn't deluge him with all the rules, I just gave him two: play the ball where it lies and play the course as you find it. Not surprising, the rest of the rules of the game are coming together. When a question arose concerning an issue of an impediment, or perhaps a need to take a drop, or any other situation where the rules must have their way, then we would take that moment and learn – always maintaining the simple and clear foundation of those first two.

There is tremendous clarity in simplicity. The Pharisees and teachers of the law burdened the people with an overwhelming number of rules and statutes, even disregarding the clear teaching of God's word to establish their own traditions.

> And he said to them, "You have a fine way of rejecting the commandment of God in order to establish your tradition! For Moses said, 'Honor your father and your mother'; and, 'Whoever reviles father or mother must surely die.' But you say, 'If a man tells his father or his mother, "Whatever you would have gained from me is Corban"' (that is, given to God) then you no longer permit him to do anything for his father or mother, thus making void the word of God by

> your tradition that you have handed down. And many such things you do." ~ Mark 7:9-13

But as I stated earlier, the Lord Jesus summed up the entire law and prophets - the whole word of God - with two simple commands: Love God and love your neighbor.

So I want you to put those two commands under your feet, stand upon them in faith and use them to evaluate everything that you plan to build in your life. Such simplicity might be hard for some because we are so wired to try and complicate matters. Why? Simple, if we can complicate them then we can control them because we invented them in the first place.

But God's word is a simple and clear rendering of His will for mankind, built upon two very solid truths: Love Him and love each other. It is in this you will discover a very powerful experience - the presence of the Father in your life. Consider the words of our Lord Jesus:

> Jesus answered him, "If anyone loves me, he will keep my word, and my Father will love him, and we will come to him and make our home with him. Whoever does not love me does not keep my words. And the word that you hear is not mine but the Father's who sent me." ~ John 14:23-24

Step onto the fairway with two simple rules: play the ball as it lies and play the course as you find it. And step into your Christian life with two very simple rules: Love the Lord your God with all your heart, mind, soul and strength and love your neighbor as yourself. You will be pleasantly surprised at how the game - and the game of life - just became a whole lot simpler.

Hole Sixteen

Self-Governed

ONE OF THE amazing things about the game of golf is that it is the only sport where the player can, and will, call a penalty on himself.

Before the re-emergence of instant replay, I was watching an NFL football game after church. The two teams were locked in dire combat, striving against each other for the win. The opposing team scored a touchdown, awarded to them by the referee. On television, however, we were able to see the slow-motion replay of the score and it was painfully obvious that the ball never crossed to goal line. But because instant replay was not a device implemented by the refs at the time, there was no going back on the score.

The coach, during his post-game interview, was asked about the "phantom touchdown." His answer shocked me, and to paraphrase it, he said something to the effect of, "What do you want me to do, forfeit the game?" His team won, that was the bottom line for him. It didn't matter how he got there or if it was even an equitable win, the victory was all that mattered.

On another day, I was enjoying a PGA tournament on television, watching fabulous shots fly across the screen. One player, in a playoff and set to make a run for victory, was near the green in a hazard. As he took his swing, he noticed a slight bit of movement out of the corner of his eye and called the rules official over to confer. After a brief moment, he took the two stroke penalty and played his next shot. No one else had noticed, but he willingly called the penalty on himself and the potential victory was snatched away with that loss of those two strokes. My friends, character counts.

There are people who live with very little, if any, self-regulation. For them, the rules are set to be broken if you can avoid getting caught; and personal character is of little value when it comes to the momentary victories or defeats in life.

And, if there were no adverse consequences to the choices made in life, I fear many more people would abandon the moral and ethical foundations and live in unregulated decay.

And that, my friends, is what is happening today. The loss of moral absolutes and the increase of sinful corruption has been normalized as lifestyle choices and perpetuated by a cry for relativistic tolerance. The spiritual deterioration that has seeped into the very fabric of our society is clearly seen with the rise of anti-Christian rhetoric and the perpetuation of what has been termed today as "political correctness."

Just because the political winds have blown our land into the sea of iniquity, does not make where we are or what we're doing any more right. Sin is still sin in the sight of God. And even if the majority of society deems a sin to be acceptable does not make it so.

Hear the warning from the Apostle Paul: "Now the Spirit expressly says that in later times some will depart from the faith by devoting themselves to deceitful spirits and teachings of demons, through the insincerity of liars whose consciences are seared" (1 Timothy 4:1-2).

There has been a searing of the conscience in the heart of mankind ever since the fall of Adam and Eve in the garden. But there is a cure!

> But when Christ appeared as a high priest of the good things that have come, then through the greater and more perfect tent (not made with hands, that is, not of this creation) he entered once for all into the holy places, not by means of the blood of goats and calves but by means of his own blood, thus securing an eternal redemption. For if the blood of goats and bulls, and the sprinkling of defiled persons with the ashes of a heifer, sanctify for the purification of the flesh, how much more will the blood of Christ, who through the eternal Spirit offered himself without blemish to God, purify our conscience from dead works to serve the living God. ~ Hebrews 9:11-14

Let us do as Hebrews 10:22 commands, "…draw near with a true heart in full assurance of faith, with our hearts sprinkled clean from an evil conscience and our bodies washed with pure water." To have your conscience cleansed requires you to draw near to God and take every thought captive. As 2 Corinthians 10:5 says, "We destroy arguments and every lofty opinion raised against the knowledge of God, and take every thought captive to obey Christ."

All of the offerings and religious efforts that we can make will not purge a defiled conscience. The sacrifice of Christ and willing submission to His salvation will. Only when you have the inner voice of your life purified by the washing of Christ will you be able to self-govern your behavior. Because, then, you will have a renewed mind.

To be self-regulated you must have a renewed mind.

Every aspect of life is touched by the corruption of sin. Your mind, your thought-life, is no different. Until your mind is renewed, transformed in the salvation of Jesus, there is no means by which you can measure whether or not your life is set to right.

I've heard it said that when you are alone, you are the real you. In a crowd, amongst the massive gatherings of humanity, people often wear a mask of acceptable behavior. But alone, in the recesses of their own life, everyone will eventually take of the mask and be completely real. I discovered this truth on the golf course as well.

I was alone. The course was sparsely populated with players and we were scattered across the various fairways with no one in sight. Working to try and improve my game, I whacked and hacked my way through the rough, from the trees and out of various hazards along the way. Suffice it to say, it was a difficult round. In the past, before this particular round of golf, I would permit myself a mulligan here and a mulligan there. My score was a reflection not of my skills on the course but of my creativity with the rules. But it never was a true reflection of my real game. I needed a mental adjustment, and I got it.

A friend and I enjoyed a cup of coffee together before I went out to play that day. We talked about the game, and he asked how mine was coming along. I told him that it was okay, nothing to brag about. Then he asked me this: "How many mulligans do you take during a round?" What? Why THAT question? "A few," I said. He grinned a little and then added, "You know, Michael, you'll never know where you really are until you are brutally honest with yourself."

He was right. My scorecard looked okay, but my game was a mess. If I were to play in a tournament with real competitors, I would never match up against them. I was not honest with myself. If I really wanted to improve my game, I needed to change my thinking – to have a renewed mind.

Paul wrote to the church in Rome and said this:

> I appeal to you therefore, brothers, by the mercies of God, to present your bodies as a living sacrifice, holy and acceptable to God, which is your spiritual worship. Do not be conformed to

> this world, but be transformed by the renewal of your mind, that by testing you may discern what is the will of God, what is good and acceptable and perfect. For by the grace given to me I say to everyone among you not to think of himself more highly than he ought to think, but to think with sober judgment, each according to the measure of faith that God has assigned. ~ Romans 12:1-3

There are many Christians who are trapped in the web of their own deceptions and unable to come to grips with the will and purpose of God in their life. They remain conformed to the world, with its lies and deceptions, embracing worldly standards as normal and finding their Christian life in a constant state of frustration because they do not have a new way of thinking.

But the transformation of your life will only come at the renewal of your mind. For, your life will always travel in the direction of your beliefs.

There is a rich promise for all who are born-again, a promise that is meant to change your thinking to bring it into conformity and harmony with the Savior. Paul illuminates this promise to us in 1 Corinthians:

> The natural person does not accept the things of the Spirit of God, for they are folly to him, and he is not able to understand them because they are spiritually discerned. The spiritual person judges all things, but is himself to be judged by no one. "For who has understood the mind of the Lord so as to instruct him?" But we have the mind of Christ. ~ 1 Corinthians 2:14-16

That final statement should fill you with great hope: We have the mind of Christ! Through the working of His grace, by the indwelling of the Holy Spirit, we are given the privilege of sharing in the thinking of Jesus, Himself. What does having the "mind of Christ" look like? Philippians will show us:

> Have this mind among yourselves, which is yours in Christ Jesus, who, though he was in the form of God, did not count equality with God a thing to be grasped, but emptied himself, by taking the form of a servant, being born in the likeness of men. And being found in human form, he humbled himself by becoming obedient to the point of death, even death on a cross. ~ Philippians 2:5-8

The one with the mind of Christ is one who is humble, will love sacrificially and is obedient to the will of the Father, faithfully doing what God commands. How is this accomplished, you ask? Good question. It comes through the Holy Spirit:

> When the Spirit of truth comes, he will guide you into all the truth, for he will not speak on his own authority, but whatever he hears he will speak, and he will declare to you the things that are to come. He will glorify me, for he will take what is mine and declare it to you. All that the Father has is mine; therefore I said that he will take what is mine and declare it to you. ~ John 16:13-15

To have a renewed mind is to live in and walk according to the truth. The Holy Spirit is the "Spirit of Truth" who will "guide you into all truth" taking from what is of Christ and making it known to all who belong to the Savior. As Paul says in 1 Corinthians 2:13, "And we impart this in words not taught by human wisdom but taught by the Spirit, interpreting spiritual truths to those who are spiritual."

A renewed mind brings new regulations.

I will freely admit that I do not know all the rules of golf. But what I do know is the spirit of the game. There is a quality to the game of golf that most who play will tell you help them to play by the rules. Simple things like "play the ball as it lies" and "play the course as you find it" eliminates much of the uncertainty and allows for a fun and competitive round. And, as I continue playing, I discover that my understanding of the game increases and my conformity to the standards improves.

Freely admitted, there is not one Christian who has ever known all the "rules" of Christianity. The entirety of the Word of God is a limitless book written by an infinite God who wants us to walk in obedience to Him. But the simple things like "love the Lord your God with all you are" and "love your neighbor as yourself" help us to keep step and walk faithfully even if we do not know all the ins-and-outs of the Christian faith. As we continue to walk with Christ, we will discover our own lives growing in greater conformity to the will of God. Or, as Paul tells the Philippians, "Let those of us who are mature think this way, and if in anything you think otherwise, God will reveal that also to you. Only let us hold true to what we have attained" (Philippians 3:15-16). God will make clear those truths that are necessary to bring about His divine purposes.

To be self-regulated requires a willingness to self-judge. Yes, I used that word "judge." God's word requires that all believers willingly stand up and be compared to the Word of God. I can almost guarantee you'll fall short, but no matter—it's the only way for you to measure your own progress. 1 Corinthians 11:31

says, "But if we judged ourselves truly, we would not be judged." Unless you're willing to judge yourself, you will never grow in the faith. Just like if you keep giving yourself mulligans along the way, your game will never improve.

There is a different standard for the believer in Christ, new regulations that you embrace and a new life that is meant to be lived. To do this you must cleanse yourself from the old life. Paul tells Timothy:

> Now in a great house there are not only vessels of gold and silver but also of wood and clay, some for honorable use, some for dishonorable. Therefore, if anyone cleanses himself from what is dishonorable, he will be a vessel for honorable use, set apart as holy, useful to the master of the house, ready for every good work. So flee youthful passions and pursue righteousness, faith, love, and peace, along with those who call on the Lord from a pure heart. ~ 2 Timothy 2:20-22

Again, the Bible says:

> But that is not the way you learned Christ!—assuming that you have heard about him and were taught in him, as the truth is in Jesus, to put

> off your old self, which belongs to your former manner of life and is corrupt through deceitful desires, and to be renewed in the spirit of your minds, and to put on the new self, created after the likeness of God in true righteousness and holiness. ~ Ephesians 4:20-24

I hold it as one of the greatest treasures of the game that most players who walk the course are honest and fair and will even call a penalty on themselves for a breach of the rules. Such should be the way of the Christian: A willingness to conform to the standards of Christ, embrace the word of God and regulate themselves accordingly.

Hole Seventeen

All Are Watching

THERE ARE EPIC moments in golf, when all eyes are watching and time stands still – frozen in that singular instant when a legend is born. Payne Stewart winning his second U.S. Open is a moment never forgotten. Who can forget Tom Watson's chip-in to win the U.S. Open over Jack Nicklaus or Tiger Woods becoming the youngest player to win the Masters? Or, better yet perhaps, is the "Golden Bear" Jack Nicklaus winning his sixth Masters at the age of 46. So many great moments are created on the field of play, and the eyes of the world are often watching.

I wonder if you've ever had a moment when you struck that perfect tee shot, made that great escape or landed a sixty-footer for birdie and then you look up and a gathered group cheered your success? Of course, you can't answer the question because you're there reading this and I'm here, perhaps thousands of miles away. But, I had a moment like that once. It was on the eighth hole of my local course.

The green stood surrounded by houses on every side. Decks and patios dressed the backside of the various homes and several of those who lived there walked among the plants and foliage of their yards. The spring day was bright and a warm sun shone faithfully upon the earth. I gave a passing hello to one elderly man who carefully trimmed a well grown rhododendron just off his porch.

I took little notice of the surround as I found my ball nestled down in the rough about ten feet off the back of the green. The greens ran fast that day and the hole was severely downhill from where I stood. I needed a good flop shot, for any chip shot would send the ball rolling right into the bunker that protected the front of the green. I opened up my sand wedge, hoping to get the ball high into the air and land soft—at least soft enough to keep it on the green.

I swung, and the club passed under the ball with the delicate precision of a neurosurgeon. High into the air, the dimpled projectile landed soft, only two feet on the green and began to roll. Slowly, revolution after revolution, the ball continued to inch toward the hole. I watched with breathless anticipation as the unthinkable happened… it went in the hole!

Suddenly, an uproar of applause echoed through the bright morning air. I turned and there behind me, gathered like a mini gallery, stood at least a dozen residents. All the people who lived in the houses around the green had come out and watched me make the chip shot of my life. I was so focused on my ball that I hadn't noticed them. But there they were – giving adulation for a shot well made. As the crowd returned to their gardens and flower beds, I heard the elderly man I had greeted speak to his neighbor with a chuckle: "Told you he'd make it."

As a Christian, your life will be forever in the sights of all who are around you. Some may immediately know that you are walking with Christ, others may see only passing glimpses of your faith. There will be those who applaud your efforts and others who will show antagonism to your love for Jesus. But the fact is you are under observation. There are always eyes upon you.

But that is actually the purpose, isn't it? The Lord Jesus says as such:

> You are the light of the world. A city set on a hill cannot be hidden. Nor do people light a lamp and put it under a basket, but on a stand, and it gives light to all in the house. In the same way, let your light shine before others, so that they may see your good works and give glory to your Father who is in heaven. ~ Matthew 5:14-16

The metaphor that the Lord uses in the text above gives clear illustration to this truth. If you ever have driven down a dark, lonely road there is such tremendous relief to see the glow of a city or town on the horizon. Anyone with children has walked in the cold dark of midnight through a living room filled with Lego landmines and is instantly grateful for a lamp that gives light to the house.

This people of this world walk a dark and lonely road. For them, you are that city on a hill - a sign of hope and refuge, a promise of safety. You are the lamp in the house, giving illumination to all who stumble about in the dark. And that illumination is seen in you. As Ephesians 5:9 describes, "For the fruit of light is found in all that is good and right and true." The goodness of your life of faith, the righteousness of Christ through you and the truth of God lived out in your life is the glowing reflection of the light of Christ. It is through such qualities that the eyes that are on you will know that you walk with Christ.

Official eyes are on you.

When you play in a tournament, there are officials who keep their eyes upon the competitors. If you watch any PGA tournaments, keep your eyes open to those who walk along with the groups and you may see the officials of the game. Certainly the camera is on the players, but once in a while you will catch a glimpse of them. And, if you play in such tournaments, you already know that the officials are on the field of play.

I've had the joy of playing in a couple of local charity events and for the most part the officials were fairly invisible. During one such event, I was a newcomer to the idea of tournament play and asked one of my competitors about the men who were following us along the fairway. "Rules official" was all my fellow player told me. We went through the entire round and only once did the official approach our group, and that was to clarify an out-of-bounds marker that looked to have been moved. But no matter how discrete they were, I knew they were always watching.

God is in heaven, and His eyes are always on you. Consider the Word spoken of King Asa in 2 Chronicles 14:2, "And Asa did what was good and right in the eyes of the Lord his God." The life that King Asa lived was seen by the God of heaven who watches over the affairs of men. I hope that it brings you joy to know that God looks down at your life, He continues to observe you.

Yet, two chapters later, Asa discovered that those eyes which looked down from heaven with joy also looked down with judgement: "For the eyes of the Lord run to and fro throughout the whole earth, to give strong support to those whose heart is blameless toward him. You have done foolishly in this, for from now on you will have wars" (2 Chronicles 16:9). Asa determined to take his own counsel and forsake the wisdom of God, and in so doing, God sent Hanani the seer to confront the king of Judah. Like facing a rules official, the king had to face the truth of his folly and he suffered the consequences of his choice.

But in the passage above, there is also a great statement of hope and encouragement - that God is looking across the whole earth to strongly support the heart set for Him. He is watching, more than just the One who enforces the rules, He is also the One who will bring strength and support to those who walk with Him.

There is one more thing that God Almighty is looking for. Jesus spoke to a woman at a well, telling her exactly who the Father is looking for: "But the hour is coming, and is now here, when the true worshipers will worship the Father in spirit and truth, for the Father is seeking such people to worship him" (John 4:23). He is looking for worshipers.

The player's eyes are on you.

When you walk upon the field of competition, you soon understand that those who play the game alongside you are also watching you play.

I played alongside a fellow competitor that was good enough to be a professional, at least from my vantage point. His shots were clean and crisp and his knowledge of the game, sharp. Along the way, he realized that I posed no serious threat to his potential win, and began to advise me as we walked. We had a marvelous time, and I found the game quite enjoyable having someone who didn't feel the need to maintain a discrete distance.

But he did call a penalty on me. I was hitting off the tee on a par three and my ball embedded in the rough just off the fairway. I lifted my ball from the mark and dropped it near the crater it made. I never considered the rule infraction, but he did. He was kind about it, told me my mistake and I took the penalty for the breach.

Unless you're on a golf team, your fellow players aren't there to help you win. They walk the course with you. Face the same potential challenges and difficulties you face. Have the same desire to win as you do. They don't get in your way and they have to play against themselves just like you play against yourself. In Christ, however your fellow "players" are there to watch you, help you, and give you what you need for victory.

One of the passages that exemplify this is found in Matthew 18. Many consider the text to be about judgment and condemnation, but it is a passage of redemption and restoration!

> If your brother sins against you, go and tell him his fault, between you and him alone. If he listens to you, you have gained your brother. But if he does not listen, take one or two others along with you, that every charge may be established by the evidence of two or three witnesses. If he refuses to listen to them, tell it to the church. And if he refuses to listen even to the church, let him be to you as a Gentile and a tax collector. ~ Matthew 18:15-17

The passage above is keyed upon the phrase: "you have gained your brother." That is, if there is genuine repentance, if he listens and you are able to bring him from the darkness of sin back to the light of Christ, you have rescued and been a part of God's deliverance for him. The other two steps concerning taking witnesses along and then telling the church are there to motivate and bring about a repentance that leads to restoration and redemption. And, then, to view him as a Gentile or a tax collector is not to abandon him to his fate but to see him as lost and needing salvation. Read the entirety of Matthew 18 and you will discover it is one of the greatest chapters on the rescue and redemption of the lost and straying soul.

Matthew 7:5 reiterates this very principle of watching your fellow Christian, "You hypocrite, first take the log out of your own eye, and then you will see clearly to take the speck out of your brother's eye." When you have removed the impediment from your own eye, then you can see clearly to help your brother with his. It implies, however, that you're paying attention.

Consider what John says in 1 John 3:17, "But if anyone has the world's goods and sees his brother in need, yet closes his heart against him, how does God's love abide in him?" To encourage one another, to help each other, to be a blessing and participate in the life of those who follow Christ right along with you requires that you are willing to paying attention.

I fear that there are multitudes of Christians who walk in this world for the sheer purpose of having someone notice them. Or, as Paul says in Philippians 2:3-4, "Do nothing from selfish ambition or conceit, but in humility count others more significant than yourselves. Let each of you look not only to his own interests, but also to the interests of others."

The gallery's eyes are on you.

Finally, the world is watching! Yes, the eyes of the world are on you and they pay very close attention to the steps – and missteps – that you make.

I think it would be a bit cruel of me to go into the litany of failed shots that I've seen in PGA tournaments. Television broadcasters can replay them for hours on end, and channels like YouTube will keep them alive in perpetuity. That, however, is not why I watch golf.

I watch the game on television because I am always learning. I watch to see great shots, to see techniques I never thought of. I watch the game because the great players are the ones on television and I still have that hunger in my heart to be great.

They have something I don't and I want to see if I can capture it for myself.

The world is watching you live your Christian life. And, yes, there is not one doubt in my mind that they are looking for the opportunity to slander, criticize and condemn the failings of the faithful who have stumbled along the way. The Psalmist experienced this very thing: "But at my stumbling they rejoiced and gathered; they gathered together against me; wretches whom I did not know tore at me without ceasing; like profane mockers at a feast, they gnash at me with their teeth" (Psalm 35:15-16). Even a quick read through the four Gospels and you encounter those who opposed Jesus always trying to catch the Lord in some trap. Mark 12:13 is just one such instance, "And they sent to him some of the Pharisees and some of the Herodians, to trap him in his talk."

But the gallery is there, the crowds of people coursing through this world, needing to see a life well lived, a faithful Christian who expresses their faith with love and grace. We've already seen that every Christian is meant to be a light in the world (Matthew 5). We have also seen that the fruit of light is goodness, righteousness and truth (Ephesians 5). These are the qualities of the Christian life that the world needs to witness through you and me.

Jesus commanded that we are to be His witnesses throughout the world: "But you will receive power when the Holy Spirit has come upon you, and you will be my witnesses in Jerusalem and in all Judea and Samaria, and to the end of the earth" (Acts 1:8). We are told to be ready with an answer for the hope that is seen in us: "…but in your hearts honor Christ the Lord as holy, always being prepared to make a defense to anyone who asks you for a reason for the hope that is in you; yet do it with gentleness and respect" (1 Peter 3:15).

When you're in a tournament, with large galleries following your every shot, it must often feel like you're playing golf in a fishbowl. Welcome to the fishbowl called Christianity! God is watching you, to give you strength and support, as well as chastisement when needed. The church is watching you, to encourage and help you along the way. And the world is watching: sometimes to mock and ridicule, yet always with a darkened eye, desperately needing the light.

Hole Eighteen

The Final Hole

THERE IS A sense of finality when you step up to the last tee box. Sometimes it's just a weekend outing with friends, sometimes it's the final hole of a four day tournament with millions on the line and a championship trophy. Granted, I've never experienced the latter event, but the former I know quite well. Even if I'm alone on the course, the eighteenth hole is the end and brings with it a mixture of emotions and thoughts.

Occasionally I arrive at the eighteenth hole exhausted and spent. I have no energy left; the last remaining shots are laborious and accomplished by the sheer force of will to finish. Other times I amble up to the eighteenth with a spring in my step, still strong and able and ready to go another round.

On one particular day, I stepped onto the eighteenth tee fully exhausted. It was hot that day, and every pore on my body was opened like the ventilation ducts in a warehouse. My eyes stung with the salty sweat that ran in small streams from beneath my hat. My sunglasses steamed in the stifling air and I was certain the earth had moved to within twelve feet of the surface of the sun. If you hadn't guessed, I was in Texas.

Now, for a man from Washington State (Western Washington State to be precise), I'm used to playing in almost all conditions – rain, fog, damp, cold, chill, even frozen conditions are the reality of being in the Pacific Northwest. However, though it gets warm up here, it doesn't get "Texas" warm! I thought about hitting my ball into the water hazard just to try and retrieve it. I knew I'd be dry three minutes after I got out.

Anyway, I slogged my way to the final hole, ready for the day of scorching misery to be over. My thoughts drifted to my wonderfully air conditioned hotel room just waiting for me, and how a tall glass of cold iced tea sounded like paradise. Then, I stepped onto the tee box.

At that moment I realized that I had come to the end of the round. Yes, it was hot. Yes, it was miserable to walk the course in the scorching solar winds. But I love the game and now this particular round was nearly over. My mind raced over all the missed shots, and my thoughts lingered on all the great ones. How I putted from just off the green to make birdie on the second hole. How, on the eleventh hole the man who I had paired up with warned me about going into the tall grasses to retrieve my ball, telling me of the potential snakes that harbored in the weeds. Despite all my whining and moaning, I actually enjoyed myself and now it was coming to an end.

But that is the way of all life. We travel around the sun, orbiting at about 67,000 miles per hour, upon a planet that is spinning at about 1,000 miles per hour and hurtling through the universe in the Milky Way galaxy that is rotating at speeds in excess of 500,000 miles per hour. Can I say it? Life moves pretty fast! The truth of the matter is you are never in the exact same universal spot, second by second. If it takes you an hour to read this chapter, you will have traveled about 568,000 miles from where you started. It doesn't feel like it, though, does it? And that is just like life. One moment you are young and vibrant, and the next, the days have nearly closed their doors. Everything comes to an end. There will be, for all of us, a final hole to play.

The book of Ecclesiastes clearly declares: "For everything there is a season, and a time for every matter under heaven: a time to be born and a time to die" (Ecclesiastes 3:1-2). In fact, the first eight verses of Ecclesiastes 3 tell the tale of all of life – a time for every activity under heaven.

Everyone must come to the end.

There is no escaping the fact that you and I will someday walk the final fairway of life. No game can continue forever and no life will continue in this world forever. I know that this seems to be an obvious truth, that everyone dies, but it is also one that is often ignored or shunted away to some castoff conversation until it's too late. But I want to tell you, even now, that this will happen to you. You will, someday, come to the end of your round and there is no escaping it. Ezekiel 18:4 states quite clearly, "Behold, all souls are mine; the soul of the father as well as the soul of the son is mine: the soul who sins shall die." And then, God would have to add this statement in the Scriptures as well: "For all have sinned and fall short of the glory of God" (Romans 3:23). Now, the math seems fairly straightforward to me. If all have sinned and all souls who sin die, then you and I are in a situation that's terminal.

Okay, open confession time. I remember once that I tried to "cheat" the course and get in a few extra holes. I had just finished the fifteenth hole and was headed to the sixteenth. However, the ninth tee box was adjacent to the sixteenth and I just casually slipped on over to the ninth instead. It looked like an easy way to get in some extra holes and play a bit longer than I should. So I carefully watched to see that no one was coming up the path, that no eye was on me and the marshal was nowhere to be seen. Then I just sauntered over and hit my shot from hole nine! Did it help? No. Was my game improved? No. At the end of it, I was simply more exhausted.

How many people try to "cheat" death? From surgeries to supplements, people across the globe will do a multitude of activities to prolong their days and try to escape the ever-encroaching moment that everyone must face. But there is no escape. Not for you or for me. The question is: what will come after? Hebrews 9:27 clearly tells us, "And just as it is appointed for man to die once, and after that comes judgment." The afterward of the final hole is the final evaluation. There will come that day when the Lord of the whole universe will sit on His throne and judge everyone. We'll cover this a bit more at the conclusion of this book, but suffice it to say, you'll need to sign your card.

Some play fast and some slow, not all games are played the same length of time.

I am, admittedly, a fast player. At my local course, if I'm first off the tee and in a driving cart, I can finish the round in less than two hours. My quickest eighteen holes was one hour and forty-five minutes! I know, eighteen holes in that short of time seems awfully quick. But if it's just me, then there's no reason to wait, no lingering over shots, and I find I actually enjoy the rapid pace of play. But I have also played in tournaments where eighteen holes seemed to take an interminable amount of time. The longest round of golf took over six hours - and that was without any weather delays! We plodded our way through the heat and humidity and finally played the last hole, simply grateful for the end.

Some lives are cut short, played fast and finished early. Others enjoy long lives and make their way to the end with patient steps. One thing the Bible tells us is that we do not know. Psalm 39:5 tells us, "Behold, you have made my days a few handbreadths, and my lifetime is as nothing before you. Surely all mankind stands as a mere breath!"

Life is a breath, a mere vapor of a moment that comes into the world and departs. Compared to the eternity that waits, the few years we have on earth is but a brief moment.

For all our days pass away under your wrath; we bring our years to an end like a sigh. The years of our life are seventy, or even by reason of strength eighty; yet their span is but toil and trouble; they are soon gone, and we fly away. Who considers the power of your anger, and your wrath according to the fear of you? So teach us to number our days that we may get a heart of wisdom. ~ Psalm 90:9-12

By this time, some might be thinking that they're already at the end. They've reached the eighteenth hole and the first seventeen have been disastrous. What can someone do, when it seems as if life has already been played, the game is nearly over?

Hope lives even at the end.

One of the things about golf that I love is, for every hole, there is hope and optimism. No matter how much the previous hole was slaughtered, no matter how many times you pitched it from the rough straight into the bunker, the next hole was coming up and there was still the opportunity for something special. Even on the last hole.

It has often been the last hole I play that brings me back to the game. On some particularly difficult days on the course, I would step up to the eighteenth tee and still hope for one last shot at redemption. And, invariably, it came. This happened at my local course not too long ago.

I had played terrible - a round of golf for the ages (the chaotic, violent and ever seditious dark ages). My scorecard looked like the mathematical formula for cold fusion and my score was high enough to win a bowling tournament. In fact, by the time I reached the seventeenth hole, I thought I should simply give up golf and take up bowling.

Long shadows cast a gloomy pall over the final fairway and even the birds had silenced their opinions. I teed up my shot, grabbed my driver and sighed. It was a short par four, just over three hundred and fifty yards and the flag was at least six shots away. I settled into my stance, took my swing and the ball sailed! I mean, it sailed straight and long. I watched it as it silhouetted against the clouds and fading sunlight. A missile launch never went truer than that shot. I walked up to my ball, forty yards from the flag and right in the middle of the fairway.

The next shot was true as well. It made the green, thirty feet from the hole. I shook my head in disbelief and sauntered up to my ball. I looked at the green; it was a downhill double-breaker for birdie. And, you know the rest of the story. I touched my putt with the finesse of a master artist laying the final brush-stroke on his masterpiece. Slowly the ball rolled, first to the right, then to the left, and then… into the hole! And, suddenly, in the flood of God's amazing grace, every other bad shot was washed away in the euphoria of that final hole.

Just because the way has been hard and the shots you've made along the way have missed the mark, you still have that final hole to play. It could be that what matters most is not how you start but how you finish. I appreciate what the prophet Joel said at God's command, "I will restore to you the years that the swarming locust has eaten, the hopper, the destroyer, and the cutter, my great army, which I sent among you" (Joel 2:25). God can restore all that was lost. You cannot go back and replay. You cannot skip back to the past and retry the bad shots you made along the way. What you must do is, from this point forward - even if it's the final hole (or even the final shot) - plan to finish well.

I met a man while I lived in Utah who was at a local rescue mission. He was a derelict in his life, broken and shipwrecked against the rocks of sin. Drugs and alcohol had claimed much of what he once was, and every shot he made up to that point was bad. When I met him, he was sixty-three years old, in a small chamber of the mission with a Bible and a book on a little desk, studying diligently the word of God. I took a particular note of him and left the mission.

About a month later I returned to speak to the gathered men. I passed that small chamber and the elderly man was gone. I inquired about him, and the mission director told me that he had gone. I thought he meant that the man had died. No. He had left the mission and moved to the Chicago area – to take on the work of his first pastorate! He made it to the final hole of his life and determined to finally play the game that God had called him to play. At sixty-three, he became a pastor for the first time. What a joy to see a man, who had once been broken and bereft of hope, to step out into the world with the message of eternal hope.

You will, someday, step up to the final hole. You will have to – everyone will. How have you played up to this point? Have you enjoyed a great round in life, serving the Lord Jesus and making great strides with the gospel? Have you made one bad shot after another and now you stand wondering if there is any hope left? Wherever you are right now, know that the final hole is coming and you must make the best of the life waiting before you.

Conclusion

Signing Your Card

YOU'VE COME TO the end of the round, played an interesting game, had some drawbacks and some successes and now it's time to enter the tent and sign your card.

Signing your card is the final evaluation, the final judgment, when the officials will say that you either made your round or you must walk off the course, disqualified. Yes... even now, it's possible to get disqualified.

How many of you have ever watched a round of golf during a PGA event and then your favorite golfer is removed from competition and is listed under the "DQ" label? They made it all the way to the final tent, signed their card and in a stunning turn of events, they were cast aside and told they failed. Why? Because they signed their card with an incorrect score.

Is it possible to find yourself at the end of your life and then, in a frightening reversal of fortunes, be cast aside from the presence of God and disqualified for heaven? In what I consider one of the most terrifying passages of Scripture, Jesus says this:

> "Not everyone who says to me, 'Lord, Lord,' will enter the kingdom of heaven, but the one who does the will of my Father who is in heaven. On that day many will say to me, 'Lord, Lord, did we not prophesy in your name, and cast out demons in your name, and do many mighty works in your name?' And then will I declare to them, 'I never knew you; depart from me, you workers of lawlessness.'" ~ Matthew 7:21-23

You may have had a great life, lived with a moral code and pursued the values and virtues of good citizenship. You may have gone to church, served on committees and participated in Sunday school from the days of your birth. You may have experienced all the wonder and joy of fellowship with God's people and even considered yourself a good person. Despite all of that, you will not be welcomed into the kingdom of Christ without knowing, and being known by, the King of kings.

So before you enter the tent of eternity, before you stand in the presence of God and "sign your card" in life, make sure you won't be disqualified when you arrive at the final judgment. Your only hope is a life surrendered to the Lord Jesus Christ. "If you confess with your mouth that Jesus is Lord and believe in your heart that God raised him from the dead, you will be saved" (Romans 10:9). Simply put, openly confess Christ as Lord (ruler of your life) and inwardly believe in the entire work of Christ through His birth, death and resurrection—conquering death for all who believe.

The reality of God's final judgment is clear in the Scriptures.

> Then I saw a great white throne and him who was seated on it. From his presence earth and sky fled away, and no place was found for them. And I saw the dead, great and small, standing before the throne, and books were opened. Then another book was opened, which is the book of life. And the dead were judged by what was written in the books, according to what they had done. And the sea gave up the dead who were in it, Death and Hades gave up the dead who were

> in them, and they were judged, each one of them, according to what they had done. Then Death and Hades were thrown into the lake of fire. This is the second death, the lake of fire. And if anyone's name was not found written in the book of life, he was thrown into the lake of fire. ~ Revelation 20:11-15

As you play your round, walking the course of your life, I implore you to make sure you do not come to the end of your days upon this earth only to find yourself disqualified.

If you are walking with Christ, when you make it to the end, though you have endured failures and enjoyed successes, you've played through the rough patches and have been out of bounds, and you stumbled through the traps and hazards along the way, know that when you arrive at the final evaluation, the Lord Jesus Christ will welcome you into His kingdom with words of victory: "His master said to him, 'Well done, good and faithful servant. You have been faithful over a little; I will set you over much. Enter into the joy of your master'" (Matthew 25:21).

It's time to play your round. Walk the course of this life with faith in Christ, hope for every moment and love in every step.

> The end of the matter; all has been heard. Fear God and keep his commandments, for this is the whole duty of man. For God will bring every deed into judgment, with every secret thing, whether good or evil. ~ Ecclesiastes 12:13-14

Now it's time to tee off. Have a great round!

For more information about Michael Duncan and his books
or to invite him speak at your event,
you can find him at his website –
http://www.authormichaelduncan.com

Made in the USA
Las Vegas, NV
27 July 2022

52235809R00132